Fleetwood Dreams

CLIMBING A MOUNTAIN
AFTER A LANDSLIDE

AMY LEIGH SAZAMA

Ten|16
PRESS

www.ten16press.com - Waukesha, WI

"Amy Leigh Sazama's *Fleetwood Dreams: Climbing a Mountain after a Landslide* unfolds in a style and voice that welcomes readers to imagine sitting together with the author as she reflects upon the challenges and tragedies of her life. She shows a path to healing through resilience and hope."
—Myles Hopper, author of *My Father's Shadow*

"*Fleetwood Dreams* takes you from agony to joy, leaving you with the feeling that no matter what goes wrong, you can make it through. Amy Sazama confronts tragedy head on, and through her words, we see her rebuilding her life one step at a time."
—Christy Wopat, author of *Almost a Mother: Love, Loss, and Finding Your People When Your Baby Dies*

"*Fleetwood Dreams* is an uplifting story of resilience, hope, and healing in the face of tragedy. Sazama combines heartbreak and humor in the perfect book for anyone who has experienced trauma and loss."
—Anna DeBakker, avid reader

"While reading *Fleetwood Dreams*, the reader can feel Sazama embrace her grief, trauma, and hardships. She brings her reader along a journey that is humorous, intriguing, terrifying, and heartbreaking. The reader quickly learns that Sazama encapsulates resiliency, growth, and most of all strength. Sazama will have you laughing out loud, picking your jaw up off the floor, and quietly shedding tears. Through this journey, Sazama teaches us how, despite hardships and tragedies, we too can overcome and live a beautiful life."
—Melissa Spellman, educator and avid reader

"What a beautiful story of love and loss. Amy uses humor and vulnerability to share her journey as she coped with hardships and learned to lean into hope and self-love. Amy tells her story with such an incredible amount of heart and grace."
—Amanda Johnson, avid reader

DEDICATION

This book is dedicated to my aunt, Mary Louise Baker;
my mom, Elizabeth Ann Daganhardt; and my daughter,
Penelope Ann Sazama.

For without all of you, I would not be.

TO MY DAUGHTER,

If you read this one day (which I hope you do), don't be afraid to share your story. Always tell your truth. Hold your head up high. Be proud and authentic. Your story is what makes you *you*. Oh, and even when this world knocks you down to your knees, get back up, stay kind, and be *hopeful*. Give life everything you've got . . . you've got nothing to lose.

Love you always,
MOM

To my readers . . . I hope you will do the same.

SHE'S GONE

I snuck out of the house the day my mom died.

She'd grounded me for typical teenage stuff (maybe I talked back, or didn't follow curfew). I don't exactly remember my misstep, but I do remember that I didn't want to accept the punishment. I followed her around the house all day long trying to convince her to unground me, but she wouldn't budge.

It wasn't usually like her to hold firm. She could be a 'softy.' There was a huge party at a classmate of mine's house that night, and everyone who was anyone was going to be there. Please excuse this shallow analogy, but in my high-school mind, this was my truth—I didn't want to miss that party.

So, once Mom was settled in for the night in front of the television, I called a friend to come pick me up and I snuck out. My sixteen-year-old, rebellious self packed a bag, grabbed a beer out of the fridge, and went quietly out the front door.

I had no idea that would be the last time I would see her alive.

Earlier in the day, my mom had broken out in hives on her arms. She hadn't made a big deal about it, just casually told me she was having an allergic reaction to something. She took an allergy pill, and that was that. I wish I had paid closer attention.

I wish I had stayed.

My plan was to attend the party for a little bit and then go to my dad's and stay the night there. My parents were divorced, so going back and forth between homes was the 'norm.' When I got to the party, I remember it not being as much fun as I had hyped it up to be. The whole night seemed to be moving in slow motion, and I had a weird feeling in the pit of my stomach. Everyone was drinking and smoking pot, and it seemed immature next to the feelings of guilt I had about sneaking out. I sat in a corner most of the night thinking about my mom and how I needed to apologize to her for not listening. Out of guilt, I left the party early and got a ride back to my dad's.

When I got there, I lied and told my dad that Mom said it was okay that I was there. I then immediately tried calling my mom. I wanted to let her know where I was and say I was sorry for leaving when I knew I shouldn't have. I wanted to ask her how she was doing. I wanted to tell her that I loved her. I called several times that night, however, I continued to get a busy signal. The longer it went without contact, the more frantic I became. After about a million busy signals, I finally decided I'd call her in the morning, and I went to sleep. I'd be able to call her in the morning, I told myself. Unfortunately, I would never get that chance.

I was woken up in the middle of the night by my dad and Eileen (my dad's girlfriend at the time), who told me that they had received a call that my mom was in the hospital. I'm not sure who called them, but I'd assumed my stepdad. Eileen said they were not told exactly what had happened, but she and my dad were told that the paramedics were able to stabilize her. When they told me that, I felt two things inside. One: Whatever happened must have been serious, and two: A sense of relief at the word *stabilize*. In my teenage mind, that sounded like a good thing. I immediately asked them to take me to the hospital so I could see her. I didn't want anything else but to see my mom and say I was sorry and that I loved her. To give her a hug and tell her that she was the best mom in the entire world.

I don't remember anything about the ride to the hospital. Nothing at all; it is all a blur. The only thing I recall about that night was that it was a frigid January night and that there was snow on the ground. It also seemed really cold getting into my dad's truck in my pajamas at 2:00 a.m. Upon arriving at the hospital, I saw my stepdad and some doctors gathered around. No one talked to me about what was happening, and everything played in slow motion again. All the adults were talking to each other to try and get information about what had happened and Mom's status. Now Auntie Mary (my mom's sister) was there too. Anyone else who may have been there is hazy at best.

I listened intently to what they were saying, but my mind raced and the words sounded all scrambled. The adults tried to get ahold of my brother, Tom. Tom was out of town working a big pressure washing job at the time, an opportunity he had been really excited about. His boss was a good friend's dad and had always been a mentor to him. Tom had been looking forward to this opportunity and making some extra money for weeks, but little did he know it would soon be cut short in the most devastating way.

At first, they couldn't reach him. His phone had been in his work truck while they were on the jobsite that day. I then decided to try and call him myself but with no luck. I wanted to talk to him so badly. I just wanted my older brother. At this moment, I declared that his five minutes older made him *much* older than me. I also officially decided that since he was older he would be *my* rock. When they were finally able to reach him, he was in a complete panic because he had twenty-plus missed phone calls. Once the news was shared with him, he and his boss immediately left and began heading back to town.

I continued to ask the adults what had happened to my mom. No one gave me any clear answers, they just explained that she would get some additional testing the next day to check her functioning. "Functioning?" I thought. "Well that's easy, she's smart, she's going to ace it!" The doctors encouraged us all to go back home and get some sleep. Once we were home, I was in complete shock. I sat straight up on the couch as my mind raced. I prayed harder than I had EVER prayed before. I even talked to my mom out loud, just as if she could hear me. I apologized to her for sneaking out earlier. I apologized to her for not being there for her through this. I told her I was really scared, and that I needed her. I begged her not to leave me. The feeling I had that night was the same feeling I had when Tom and I were told that my parents were getting divorced. It felt like the rug was ripped out from underneath me again. The feeling of immediate uncertainty.

I didn't want to sleep alone, so I curled up and slept at the bottom of my dad's bed. I squeezed my eyes shut tight and tried so hard to sleep, but I remember frequently waking up and asking if my mom would be okay. The answer I heard over and over again was "Yes, she will be okay. Everything will be okay. Try and sleep." I also remember waking up in a panic sometime closer to morning because I had a very vivid dream about my mother. She was so beautiful in my dream. She had a bright light surrounding her. Angelic, really. She seemed so happy and loving. She told me she was not mad at me for anything at all. She told me that she loved me. That I was an amazing daughter. That I brought joy to her. She also said, "Goodbye."

I jumped up after my dream and demanded to go back to the hospital. The adults could not get ready fast enough. I sat and waited in the truck. "They better hurry," I thought to myself. "I need to see my mom!" Tom finally got to the hospital that morning too. Thank God, because the news wasn't good. They did the scan. It turns out Mom didn't ace it like I thought. She had no brain activity. None at all. Hours had now passed, and the adults had decided after speaking with the doctors they were going to take her off life support. I still couldn't comprehend what any of this meant, and I just remember feeling very scared. I kept asking what had happened to her, and Tom and I were only told that her heart had stopped working. I now know that if her heart had actually stopped working, she wouldn't have been hooked up to machines. That she would already be gone. That is the narrative we believed, though. In essence, they were trying to soften the blow for us. Simplify what had really happened. Protect us.

Everything finally became real when my aunt Mary walked with me toward my mom's room and encouraged me to say my goodbyes. I walked in and stood there for a moment. I then lay right next to my mom in the hospital bed and began to sob.

"Please come back," I begged her. "You're the best mom in the entire world. I'm so sorry for anything bad I have ever done." Lying next to her, I had flashbacks of her cooking dinners, coaching my soccer games, driving me to and from cheerleading practice, seeing her in the audience at my choir concerts, school plays, and basketball games, her helping me pack for Girl Scout Camp, taking me to Parks and Rec, and her playing with my hair and scratching my back at night when I couldn't sleep. I also remembered how she looked when she smiled proudly to others while introducing me as her beautiful daughter, and boasting about me even when I failed at something. I remembered her relentless hope, and her keeping us all afloat during the hard times. I could have sworn she squeezed my hand, but I'll never know. That was the last time I would see her. I didn't want to leave, but I had to. And when I finally did leave that room, I would leave *Motherless*.

Eventually, I had to leave her room. Like a scene in a movie, I leaned up against a wall and slid back down it while crying. I then put my head in my hands and sobbed. A random stranger came up to me and asked if I was okay. She was middle-aged with dark hair and smiling innocently as she asked me this question. Her smile at the time, while comforting, was also annoying. Why was she smiling when my mom just died?! I looked at her and announced straight-faced, "No, I'm not okay. My mom's gone. She just died." Now I felt like I could throw up. She came up behind me and touched my shoulder for quite some time. She didn't leave. She stayed there and just listened to me cry. She didn't seem so annoying anymore. She seemed motherly, and that I wanted. That I needed. My mom was now gone, and I'd take this stranger and 'motherly moment' for as long as it would last. Eventually, when it became dark, I had to leave that hospital. Leaving the hospital meant I was abandoning my mom, something I never once imagined I'd have to do.

Mom's funeral was a total zoo. People were lined up out the

door into the parking lot of the funeral home. That part I liked. It reminded me that she was loved. Mom always had a beautiful trait of rooting for the underdog in life, and this was the moment I saw how many underdogs in the world there really are. This was the moment they had come to say "thank you" to her. "Thank you for helping me when no one else would. Thank you for seeing me when no one else did. Thank you for making me feel like a somebody when others made me feel like a nobody. I'll miss you." I remember sitting on a bench staring off at a wall as people came up to me to express their condolences. I also recall people asking me how I was doing. This seemed funny to me at the time, as it felt like a trick question. Nothing seemed real. Time again, moving in slow motion. This time even slower than before.

Aunt Mary got up and spoke about Mom. Tom and I were sitting next to one another shoulder to shoulder by this time. We had moved to the second row from the first, because the front row seemed too close, too real. Dad was nearby too. He looked pale and a bit lost. Out of place even. Aunt Mary got up to the podium at the front of the room and spoke about my mom's kindness, her huge heart, her loving nature, her beauty, and how she lit up a room. She talked about her being an amazing mother, friend, sister, and aunt. I remember thinking to myself, in that moment, that I wanted to be like that. I wanted to be like her.

When the funeral was over and all the dust had settled, Tom and I were given the choice to continue living with our stepdad and stepsiblings or go live with our dad. We both decided that we wanted to go live with our dad. Back then, it felt like a fresh start. Being by Dad also reminded us of happier times when we were younger. Times when life seemed lighter, more innocent, and fun. Where there seemed to be more *hope*.

Tom and I made a pact that whatever we did, we'd stick together. So, less than a week or so after Mom died, we both uprooted and started living at our dad's house permanently. There was no formal goodbye or big moving day. Maybe that's because that time in my life is a haze, or maybe we just unenthusiastically *left*. I left all my bedroom furniture, only grabbing my clothes and special belongings. I also don't remember saying goodbye to my stepdad or stepsiblings. We just kind of quietly exited and started over.

From that day on, I was different. I no longer felt sixteen, but much older. My bubbly spirit was still there, but it didn't come as naturally anymore. I'd have to force it. I'd begin searching and thinking about how this could happen to *her*. How this could happen to *my mom*. I'd also reflect on her death and how it would have many lasting effects, and change lives. To piece it all together, though, I'd have to go back to the beginning. I'd have to go back to the start.

THE START

It's funny how your 'life lens' as a child looks so much different than when you're an adult. Have you ever gone back to a certain place you frequented as a child when you're older, and things just look so much smaller? Maybe they lack the wonder and vibrant colors you saw as a child. Maybe they smell differently or just simply seem a lot less magical. Maybe their mundane, gray qualities stand out and pierce your soul in an undeniable way, and the laughter and sweet voices from the past leave you with nothing but a haunted feeling.

There's just so much hope in our world when we're little. We trust people. We see life's beauty. We truly believe things are going to work out okay and that things will stay this beautiful forever. We latch onto those souls around us who make us feel safe, and we believe that they will always be with us. Our hearts are free, our minds are wild, and our love flows freely like a waterfall. Then one day, something happens and those glasses fall off. The magic dissipates, and we see things for how they truly are. We might remember this moment, or maybe it happened without us even knowing.

That's the moment when, for the rest of our lives, we do everything we can to try and find those glasses and put them back on. At thirty-seven years old, I now believe those glasses symbolize *hope*. Something we had when we were born, stayed with us when we were small, and then somewhere down the line . . . was something we had to search for, we had to find. For me, I do remember when those glasses fell off and broke into a million little pieces. But before I go there, you have to see how beautiful things were. How magical and loving. How much potential there was. You also have to know that no matter how fragmented, hazy, and busted those glasses have become, I still find a way to wear them proudly.

FLEETWOOD

We grew up on a street you would see in a Norman Rockwell painting. The houses were cute and quaint, and the people on the street were not just neighbors, but friends. We lived in a two-story white house with black shutters and a white picket fence that my dad proudly built. A perfect start to the picturesque American Dream. Across the street lived my aunt Mary (my mom's sister). Always just one big wheel ride away, she had perfectly styled thick brown hair, a sweet smile, and a high-pitched voice with a contagious, silly laugh. She was always my mom's closest friend as well as a constant growing up for both my twin brother Tom and me. She also wasn't afraid to help my mom change a diaper, or *ten*.

Down the street, you had one of my best friends, Courtney, and her family. Courtney was a year younger than me and especially energetic and limber. Her parents put her in gymnastics at an early age, and I remember she was always wearing colorful gymnastic leotards and doing cartwheels and back handsprings during conversation. I always secretly wished my parents had put me in gymnastics too, so I could have the cool jacket she wore proudly with the name of her gym on it. I always felt that it increased her status a smidge.

Courtney had an older brother, Kevin, who was one year older than my brother and me. Tom became friends with Kevin, and me with "Court." Kevin and Courtney's parents were still married and had the type of marriage you could only wish to grow old and find. Her mom was a nurse (my mom frequently called her for medical advice when my brother and I even sneezed once), and her dad did something with insurance I believe. He looked important because he was always dressed nicely when he returned home from work. He doted on Courtney's mom in the most endearing way and was always present (the way I would end up wishing my dad had been).

Across the street to the left of my aunt Mary, you had the Hansley family. My other best friend, Mya, lived there. Mya was one year older than me. She was an only child with the most beautiful blonde curls. Everyone was always telling her parents how 'stunning' she was. She was wise and intuitive beyond her years, and very serious as a child. Most of the time that I got in trouble in my childhood, it was with Mya. We liked to conspire together. She definitely liked to push the limits, and I loved going to her house because her mama, Jean, spoiled us both. We also got anything we wanted to eat per Mya's request, which when you're little feels a bit like winning the kid lottery.

Then you had Richard and Robbie (Robbie a piano teacher and Richard an artist of some sort). They were very eclectic in their own right. Richard was exceptional at sketching quick cartoon-like drawings on the spot per request, and Robbie was sweet, nurturing, and protective. A babysitter of ours once threw a party at our house while sitting. Tom and I were okay with it, as Tom, being a smart-ass business-minded six-year-old at the time, propositioned some candy and a late bedtime out of a deal to not tell our parents. Robbie called our mom the next day anyway to let her know the unfortunate party news. Mom was grateful for the call, and we never saw that sitter again. For the record . . . Tom told too.

There were also some nice elderly couples sprinkled in the mix, a woodworker who made my brother and me hand-painted turtle stools so we could reach the bathroom sink, some guy my dad used to throw the football around with during half-time of the football games, a principal and his wife, and a few other background people who were necessary in the Norman Rockwell painting lineup, but not necessarily strong enough to play a key part. Background noise, if you will.

There you have it. Frame Avenue . . . 140 Frame Avenue where 'hope glasses' are worn daily with your mismatched kid clothes, neighbors are your best friends, doors stay unlocked, snow days are legendary, footballs are thrown, and fun memories are made night and day. There are no broken homes (yet), no murder (yet), no drugs (yet), no heartbreak (yet), and no sleepless nights wondering how things could have played out differently. You feel warm inside like you're wrapped in a cozy, soft blanket. Where your family dog even has a hopeful name. Chance we'd call him.

There's a soundtrack to my childhood. A memory that I return to over and over, a record on repeat . . . It's Christmas Eve in the late '80s and my parents are in their late twenties. My mom resembles Goldie Hawn, with her fluffy, layered blonde hair, tan skin, and a beautiful, white smile, and my dad resembles Kurt Russell, handsome, tall, charismatic, muscular, and funny. A true ladies' man, if you will. Flirtatious they were. Quirky and full of love for us and each other. Like two hopeful teens in love. They were always laughing together. Dad, the goofy one, prided himself in making Mom smile.

Mom, Dad, Tom, and I are all setting up the Christmas tree together. My parents have the new Fleetwood Mac *Rumours* album blasting on repeat in the background, and ornaments and tinsel are spread out all over the oatmeal-colored carpet. Tom and I (around five at the time) are in matching boy/girl robes (over our pajamas), holding hands and swinging each other in circles, laughing hysterically as we let go unannounced so the other goes flying backward (preferably into a wall) for entertainment purposes. We all take turns putting ornaments on the tree, attempting to make this year's tree look more studious than the last, with Chance watching intently, as though proud to claim us as his family.

Life seemed good. Life seemed really, really good.

HOLY SH*T THERE'S TWO

We were born in Waukesha, Wisconsin (America's Dairyland), known for a few essential things. Here they are in no particular order: beer, cheese, farms, freezing cold winters, snow, family, church, the Green Bay Packers, and the proud home of Les Paul where the electric guitar was born. One could say we had it all!

Both of my parents were born into the Catholic faith, and both families prided themselves in continuing the tradition of putting their children in private Catholic schools. The two of them met in a Catholic high school located in their hometown. From what I've heard, my mom was beautiful and quite popular in high school. She was on the poms dance team, and guys were calling the house and asking her on dates regularly. I found out later in life that this is how my aunt Mary met her first husband. My aunt later told me how he would call the house asking for Liz, who was never home, and they got to talking. Early on, my mom was always 'the one who got away.'

During their school years at Catholic Memorial, my dad

admired my mom from afar. She was the pretty prize he was always after. One day, he finally built up enough courage in his shy, little body to ask her to prom. Mom later told me she only went with him because he asked her first, and it was the 'right thing to do.' His well-maintained status of class clown must have helped him out a little too. My dad was visibly shorter than her (which bothered him), and a bit awkward and apprehensive at the time. I'm pretty sure he even had a slight lift on his neatly polished black dress shoes to give him an extra inch or two. He settled on wearing a brown bow tie with a baby blue suit coat to prom that day. He also rocked a brown shag with crooked bangs, and he wrapped his arm around her for that prom picture like it was 'proof.'

After prom, my parents briefly stayed in contact throughout their school years, passing each other in the halls and periodically waving hi to one another. But, they didn't end up dating until after my dad returned home from college a few years later. According to my mom, when he came back, she almost didn't recognize him because he was now a total heartthrob. He had grown several inches taller during his college career at UW–River Falls (now reaching over the six-foot mark). He still had his brown shag, but this time it made more sense. During college, he thrived in his fraternity and bartending job and played the ladies like he was getting back at them.

The night he was back in town, my mom was out playing pool with a friend of hers at a local pub in their hometown, when in walked Gary. Tall, confident, handsome, muscular, and funny. His style had improved significantly by then too. She never told me, but in my mind, I imagine him wearing a flannel shirt, a tight (but not too tight) pair of slightly faded dark jeans, and cowboy boots like he always did when we were growing up. He'd have a rugged look to him and exude a bit of a 'bad boy' vibe with a beer in one hand and a lit cigarette in the other. She once told me that her heart skipped all sorts of beats that night, and the rest was pretty much history. These two lovebirds got married, moved into a small apartment together, and became pregnant. This is where I come in.

Dad was working at the concrete company my grandfather started from the ground up. Grandpa poured his heart and soul into this business, as he came from a background of thirteen brothers and sisters and literal dirt floors. He worked hard, and he taught my dad to do the same. After my dad's brief stint selling copy machines, my grandparents decided he could come work for the family business. He'd had one major successful moment in copy machine sales after landing a huge job in Milwaukee because someone thought he looked like the Marlboro Man. After that all-star, shining moment, though, he ended up working for the family concrete business for good.

My dad was out working on a jobsite the day my mom ventured out to her first doctor's appointment to get a little glimpse at the precious baby growing inside of her. While there, her doctor shared the news that there was not just one, but two of us! My mom couldn't believe it. She was scared, overjoyed, and in total shock. She even called my aunt Mary because she needed to say it out loud to someone just to believe it. They shared in the excitement and immediately started planning out everything she would need for 'the twins' (this would now be what we were called from the womb on). She then called my dad's work, and Grandma answered the office phone. This was my grandma's secretarial duty along with writing the paychecks to the workers.

Sometimes she'd answer with "Concrete Placement Company," and other times she'd just shout into the phone, "Yeah?" When she picked up, my mom gave her the news and made her promise not to tell my dad. She reluctantly agreed.

Grandma immediately got off the phone and two-way radioed my dad, who was out on a jobsite laying concrete. "Gary, have you talked to Liz today?!"

"No, why?!" he asked.

"Never mind, I can't tell you!"

When Dad got home from work later that day, Mom told him the news, and they celebrated together. They were thrilled and, according to my dad, equally as terrified. They were in it together, though, and according to my parents and the Beatles, they were good because "All You Need Is Love," right?

BOY/GIRL TWINS

Here's the thing I've come to learn about twins as I've gotten older. To generalize, I feel like you get one of each kind. One of the twins is more outgoing, maybe a bit funnier or louder, takes the lead, and is more protective of the other. The other twin is a bit more shy, maybe more sensitive, and is completely okay letting their twin pave the way for the both of them. I was the shy one. I hid behind Tommy. I let him take the lead because he made me feel safe and protected. He would feel out the room and let me know when it was time to come out. My dad even made up a song about us when we were still growing in my mom's womb together, a song demonstrating Tom's early signs of protectiveness of me. He'd sing it around the house, and it would echo through the halls, "You can get my brother but you can't get me, bah da da dum, I'll hide behind his left kidney." Tom was the yin to my yang, and when you put us together, we made absolutely perfect sense.

My parents settled on naming us Tom and Amy, after ditching their original choices of Jessica (Jessie) and James after they remembered that Jesse James was an American outlaw and bank and train robber back in the 1800s. Although we *did* conspire *a lot* together, so perhaps their first choices weren't too far off. I'm not exactly sure where Tom's name originated from, but Dad once told me they named me Amy after a popular girl in their high school who was 'bubbly' and 'always nice' to everyone she came in contact with. I always thought that was a ridiculous reason, but I think after finding out, I've always tried to live up to my given name. I *did* like how my parents picked three letters for both names, though, as I thought it flowed nicely.

Tom and I were inseparable from the get-go. He was my built-in best friend, born just five minutes before me, and he always made sure people knew that part. Every new person Tom would meet, he would stand up tall and proclaim that he was the older one of the two of us. I always wanted to blurt out, "Only by five minutes!" but I always let him have his glory. My parents told us when we were first born, they would put us on opposite ends of our crib and somehow we would shimmy towards one another and sleep as closely to each other as we could. They couldn't figure this out since we were still so little and immobile. They experimented with this, though, night after night. They would put us on opposite ends of the crib, and when one of them would come in to check on us, we were right there next to each other with our heads touching. They were in complete awe.

When we were still in diapers, the time we were both most playful and content was when my parents would lay us down on a blanket next to each other on the floor. Around the age of a few months old, we would roll around together grabbing our feet, smiling, and exuding peace and happiness. We quickly started to do everything together. We learned to crawl together, walk together, tasted our first bites of real food together, and potty trained together. We even had bunk beds and shared a room for a little while together. We occupied the same room until around the age of five. We slept in those bunk beds, and Tom would holler down all the 'rules of the room' from the top bunk because he was always in charge.

He dropped a quarter down once and convinced me to swallow it. I did. He told me to hide in a dresser drawer before bed so our parents couldn't find me and start our bedtime routine. I did that too. He even threw up (or down) from the top bunk once because he wasn't feeling well . . . just missing me by inches. I went running down the stairs that night, yelling out to my parents that "Tom blew up." It wasn't until the third time of me repeating this that my parents realized I was trying to report that "Tom threw up." Tom found the whole night wildly funny, but even with all the twin chaos, we loved sharing a room. So much so, that when my parents finally had an addition put on the house (so we could each have our own bedroom), we could still only be found in one room.

Tom was different even as a child. My parents used to tell us that I was as limber as a Raggedy Ann doll. People would pick me up, and I would become flimsy and melt into their arms like putty. I didn't cry or fuss much, and I was always watching everything around me inquisitively, especially Tom. Tom was unlike this, though. He was always tightfisted. He was not flexible, and he cried a lot. He was pretty colicky as a baby. When you picked him up, he would stiffen up and clench his fists up tightly.

Tom had sandy blonde hair and was shorter than me for most of our childhood, which pissed him off because people were always asking us to stand next to one another to compare.

In moments of Tom's despair about his height, my dad promised him he would sprout up in college like he did, but this wasn't very helpful to him from elementary through high school.

My first-grade teacher quietly pulled me aside once and told me that Tommy reminded her of Ralphie from *A Christmas Story*, and I'd say that was a pretty accurate description. He wore thick, brown-framed glasses throughout his early school years, which my parents constantly had to replace because he kept losing them. Turns out, he buried all his glasses one by one in the backyard garden so he wouldn't have to wear them. The only reason my dad stumbled upon the gigantic stockpile of glasses one day is because Chance dug them all up. The kid definitely had character.

When Tom was in upper elementary school, he was diagnosed by his pediatrician with ADHD, and he would also grow to suffer from horrible migraines. The type of unbearable migraines where you have to lock yourself in a room and turn off all the lights for the day. My mom would get phone calls from school and have to pick him up early because his headaches would be so bad that he needed to come home and lie down in the pitch-dark just to feel better. Back then, my mom didn't know much about ADHD or the cause of his migraines. ADHD wasn't a diagnosis that was as freely talked about as it is today, and they could never quite figure out what triggered his headaches.

The doctors only told my mom to give him a little caffeine to help, so he would get a piece of chocolate or two from time to time. It didn't help, but he never turned down chocolate. She did her best to advocate for him and try to get more answers, but she never really got any solid ones. I think this contributed to him acting out sometimes. I also think this is why Mom excused his behavior. I didn't understand any of this growing up, I just knew that Tommy had more doctor's appointments than I did.

Tom also had a bad bout of spinal meningitis when he was a kid. I don't remember his exact age, but I know it was in his toddler years. I recall him being very sick and ending up needing to stay in the hospital for a couple of nights. Aunt Mary came over to stay with me. I also recollect my parents being *absolutely terrified.* He pulled through, but there was a brief moment in which my parents didn't know if he would. They later found out that he caught it from a neighborhood girl at a birthday party we were invited to. My mom talked about this event for years to come. I'm not sure if it had any lasting effects on him, but back then he seemed fine. Growing up, he liked to tell this story in a superhero kind of way, with his chest puffed out, as if he was proud he had dodged death.

Another thing about Tommy is that he was always making people laugh (especially me). This was *HIS* superpower. Just like my dad, he got through school by being a class clown. He could make *anyone* laugh, even the teachers when they weren't supposed to. Tom was almost always immediately eyed up and chosen to sing solos in our school concerts. He was so lively and funny, and it made for great entertainment. I even remember him singing "Feliz Navidad" in an Elvis voice in our elementary school Christmas concert. He stood on stage singing confidently while waving his hands in the air, with a huge self-satisfied grin on his face. I'm pretty sure he even got a standing ovation at the ripe-old age of six.

My mom always had a soft spot for Tom. I'm not *exactly* sure why, but her love for him was *very* deep. I often thought that she loved him just a little more than me. I was okay with this, though. I always felt like he needed more love.

Anyway, I was a daddy's girl growing up. I followed Dad around our house, watching him do projects every weekend. Dad would start a project and stay up all night just to finish it. He had tunnel vision when it came to projects, as he liked to build something with his hands and stand back to see the finished product. Like many little girls, I held my dad on a pedestal. He was my hero. I was always watching him intently for life's answers because, in my little mind, he had them all.

Dad was a hard worker. I think he liked working in concrete because when you think about it, it's just one project after another. Every night, my dad would come home smelling like cigarette smoke, concrete, and gasoline. The aromas of the shop he worked in, and the aromas (to me) that symbolized determination. I still love the smells of gasoline and Marlboro Lights because of the memories and nostalgia that come with them. I also *never* walk on wet cement to honor all the hard work I know goes into laying and finishing a sidewalk.

He never failed to tell us or show us the Concrete Placement Co. stamp to look out for on the work he and my grandpa did around town. City contract after city contact they would do. First, my grandpa and then my dad when he took over the company later on in life.

HE LOST AN EYE

One thing I believe is that trauma is generational and can change the trajectory of everything. Trauma has to go somewhere. I believe it stays in our cells and is passed down from generation to generation until it is dealt with completely and fully.

My dad, Gary Lee Tegge, was the middle of three born to Robert and Harriet Tegge. He was a wild one, even as a child. I'm pretty sure he lived out his childhood pretending he was the main character of an old Western movie. According to my grandma, he was mischievous and always stirring up some kind of trouble. He was an underdog in many respects. He was small and he only had one working eye (I'll get to this in a minute). He spent much of his childhood having surgeries on his eye, and due to this found a sense of humor that would carry him throughout his school years.

Dad was born with two working, bright blue eyes, and by all accounts was a pretty normal, healthy kid. Unfortunately for him, though, his fate would change. One weekday, my grandma took my dad and my uncle Bobby over to her sister's house to play with their cousins and a few neighborhood kids. The sisters were sitting on some folding chairs in the backyard, soaking their feet in one of those small plastic kids pools to stay cool—talking amongst themselves in their exaggerated, excessively hand-gestured, loud, Italian sort of way (I mean that in the best possible manner)—when they heard blood-curdling screams coming from a small garage next door.

My grandma raced off of her folding chair and into the garage where my dad was holding his left eye, sobbing. He was two at the time. At first, she didn't quite know what had happened. Once she saw my dad's eye, though, she immediately ran inside with him and began flushing it out. It turns out my dad and the kids were playing in the run-down garage when one of the older kids grabbed a stick and was knocking bottles down off a shelf for fun. Well, one of those bottles had acid in it. The acid fell, splashed back up off the dirty garage floor, and hit my dad square in his eye. "Bullseye," as my dad would later say every time he recounted the story.

The doctors at the hospital initially said he would be alright, and my grandma felt very relieved. The next day, though, my grandpa went in to check on him, and his eye was glued shut. He was eventually diagnosed as blind in that eye and would require countless surgeries. He told me stories about how he would stay in Chicago all by himself for the weekend having surgery on his eye. His only real pleasure while he was there was a vending machine down the hall from his room where he would buy candy that he wasn't supposed to eat before surgery. He also looked forward to my grandpa visiting with him on Sundays.

The surgeries were a bit experimental, as they were just

coming out with the prosthetic lens at the time. During surgery, they would scrape the scar tissue from his eye to have him fitted for a new prosthetic lens. Apparently, the doctors were always dangling the carrot in front of my grandpa that just maybe his clouded-over, blind eye could eventually be fixed. Perhaps that is why my grandpa was so successful at business. Aside from being an innately hard worker (working his way up from absolutely nothing), maybe he was saving up for an eye to fix my dad. Truth be told, though, the trauma my dad experienced that day from losing his eye changed the trajectory of many lives.

Why would one left eye change lives? My grandma had a lot of feelings about that day. Maybe some guilt, maybe some anger at herself or my dad, and maybe some fear because I'm sure eye fixin' isn't cheap. The surgeries and appointments he would eventually need would add up. My dad was treated differently growing up. The way I always understood it was that he was an annoyance to her. A problem that couldn't be fixed. A trouble-maker. She would say black, so he would say white. She couldn't be there for my dad the way he needed her to be. She showed her love for him by buying things. She attempted to make up for it later in life by buying him even more.

This was traumatic for Dad. Not just losing his eye, but the way he felt growing up. He felt insignificant and small. He never quite felt like he could be good enough, and he started to act out for attention. He knew he wasn't her favorite, and at times that made him go the complete opposite way. He often used his humor to deflect from the pain he endured when he was a child, but it was hard, and it left its mark. The only good to come out of it was that his struggles would also shape him to become sensitive, funny, rebellious, and a bit of a scrapper at times. He's always fought his way through life like a scrappy raccoon claiming its turf.

When he later met my mom and wanted to ask her to marry him, he knew he would have to show her his glass eye lens and fill her in on his childhood traumas. One night while trembling and terrified, he told her that he had to show her something. My mom was scared. She had no idea where this conversation was going to lead, what he was about to say, or even if it would be a deal-breaker. He quickly took his eye (lens) out and held it in his hand, waiting patiently for her to respond. She stared at him directly in the other eye, smiling, and said, "Gary, I've known about this since we were in high school."

Dad, looking confused, and a bit humiliated, quickly put his eye back in and fumbled with his words for a minute. It was awkward for a moment or so, but she didn't let him stumble for long. She kept her sweet, pretty grin and suggested that the two of them name it. They laughed and decided on "Gizmo." That was the type of person my mom was. Throughout their marriage, she would occasionally find it in the couch or on the bed mattress, hand it to him, smile, and tell him to "Quit losing Gizmo."

Coincidentally, that eye also became a bit of a game for Tom and me too. When Dad had his prosthetic lens in, his eye wouldn't close all the way when he slept, so we never knew if my dad was actually sleeping or not. Tom and I would jump up and down and wave our hands in front of him when we were kids, trying to see if Dad was actually sleeping or not. If he didn't blink, we knew we could turn on the shows we weren't allowed to watch when he was awake. He always chuckled when we told him this in the morning.

My dad told me that they could never fix his broken eye and put a new eye in because our bodies remember the original trauma that occurred, and the eyes can't quite adjust right. I looked it up, and sure enough, it's true. And just as I mentioned above, our bodies always remember trauma because it has to go somewhere. And if it's not worked through, it can cause generational ripples.

A BAD BREAK

My mom, Elizabeth Ann Daganhardt, was the oldest of three born to Dorothy and James Keyes. She was a bit of an outdoorsy, free spirit even as a child and was always rooting for the underdog (a trait she carried into her adult life). To this day, I know exactly the souls she would have targeted to find a way to make them feel good about themselves. She was kind, beautiful, and lit up any room she walked in. She was protective of her siblings and made the most of her broken childhood. Her dad was an abusive alcoholic who targeted her the most. From stories I've heard, she took this abuse and tried to protect the younger ones the best she could.

Even if your family is incredible on all accounts, I think we've all looked at another family before and thought, "I wonder what it would be like if they adopted me?" In my heart, I have to believe that my mom had to think this a time or two when she was growing up. Or daydream about running away.

Since she was the oldest child of three, my grandma was a bit strict with her. Her hair had to be cut very short, her nails needed to be perfectly manicured, Catholic schooling was a must, and Sundays were for dressing nice and church. Add piano lessons, horseback riding, and homework into the mix, and now you have a glimpse into my mother's childhood. I know that my grandma (an Irish English teacher) was teaching my mom what she too had learned was important, but the problem was that my mom didn't feel comfortable going to her mom with the 'hard stuff.' The truly hard stuff that children need to feel comfortable to talk to their parents about. The *real* problems.

Aside from the normal stuff, like puberty, strangers, the birds and the bees, and the drug and alcohol talk, another topic my mom didn't feel comfortable talking to her mother about was her father. He was always a taboo, uncomfortable subject, even for me. A subject you put in a box and close the lid tight. My mom would often look at me and say, "You're too young for me to tell you now, but remind me to tell you something when you're older." She would also frequently say, "Always tell me if someone is hurting you." There would then be an awkward pause, and I would eventually respond, "I will, Mom. I know."

I would later find out that she was badly abused by her father. He would drink until the point of blacking out and abuse her. Even writing this feels scary and icky to me. It feels like someone may come out of the walls and scold me. This has been such a forbidden subject in my family for so long that it feels like I'm touching a scalding, hot stove. Like I want to look around and make sure no one is watching me so I know it's safe. I have to talk about it, though. I have to talk about it *for* my mom. You can't keep trauma hidden in a box in the back of a closet because then it hurts and haunts you. I also believe it haunts your children and your children's children until the secret knocking at the door is finally let out.

It affected so much of who she was as a person. When I say she didn't want others to hurt, it's because she knew deep pain. This is why she was always rooting for the underdog. This is why she didn't ever see how truly beautiful she was.

Someone else's dad took her to the father/daughter dance at her school. I saw a picture of it once. It made me sad. She longed for a father figure. One she could lean on, one she could trust. Thankfully, she ended up becoming very close to my grandpa (her father-in-law), even calling him "Dad." Not just because that's what in-laws do, but because she wanted to. He loved her the way a dad should, and she loved him like a daughter would. Their relationship was fun, playful, and light, something that had been unfamiliar to her growing up. She craved to be loved. She also had a vulnerability about her. I can't quite describe it. It's the same vulnerability that made her beautiful, yet deeply broken at times. She carried with her a secret. A dark, heavy, cloudy secret.

My grandmother eventually found the courage to divorce my grandfather. It wasn't easy on her. She told me this story many times growing up, and about the hardships that came along with it. In her mind, this act was courageous, hard, and heroic. Divorce was uncommon back then, especially for devout Catholics. She also now had to support and raise three girls all on her own. She eventually stopped teaching and started her own magazine-distributing company called Midwest Magazine Services.

With her new business, she could now work from home and support her daughters. She leaned heavily on the church and her two best friends ('the nuns' as she would later refer to them). They were Catholic nuns who showed up randomly here and there at our family functions. Our family all grew to know and love them. They helped my grandma through the hard times and helped her to get back on her feet. I will say, though, we got some strange looks when we were out in public with them as kids. People would look, stare, and point when they were dressed in their full coverings and head veils. Tom and I would giggle.

I always felt close to my grandma. She taught me that women can be strong, independent, and support themselves. She also taught me to be disciplined. She was very intelligent, and one of the strongest women I knew. I was asked to help take care of her during her final years. I'd run errands for her, paint her nails, clean her room at the nursing home, brush her hair, and watch the Green Bay Packers football games with her. One day, she even gave me money and asked me to shop for the "prettiest smelling perfume" I could find for her. She wanted to feel young and special again. She also told me to buy myself a bottle. When I got back with the perfume, we sprayed ourselves and she asked me to style her hair. I could tell, for that day, she found a little bit of her youth again. These memories I cherish to this day.

As for my grandpa, he eventually sobered up later in life and apologized to my mom for the damage he had caused. Unfortunately, it was too late. At least that's what I say while standing up tall and strong in my mother's corner. They slowly started to build a relationship in her early twenties after we were born. Unfortunately for him, though, he was diagnosed with lung cancer during this time and passed away. My aunt Mary took care of him while he was sick, and my mom and dad would walk across the street to her house to visit. I guess he did get to meet Baby Tom and me too. He told my mom he was proud of her and that he thought we were "so cool."

However, because of what happened to my mom, she *always* craved a father's love, and it caused her to choose the wrong men at times. It normalized behavior she should have never accepted because it was wrong and, quite frankly, she was just too good for it. She deserved more. She deserved a better start and a *normal* childhood. One she didn't have to fear or that forced her to grow up too quickly. Because of what I now know of my mother's childhood, I believe that she had the burden to work twice as hard to break unhealthy family cycles and do better for herself and her children. I'm proud of her. She really gave it her best shot.

START MAGIC CAR

When I was a kid, my parents had a 1980 bronze-brown Bronco that (for its total net worth, which wasn't much) my dad kept meticulously clean. It was a real beaut, but the problem was it didn't always like to start on the first go-around. My dad was really proud of that car. He always had a habit of buying unique vehicles that looked like you were headed straight to a campsite for a weekend fun excursion. I'm not sure, though, that he knew how many times it wouldn't start when Mom needed to drive us to school in the morning.

The mornings would start out pretty smoothly, aside from the typical kid stuff like arguing about what was weather-appropriate to wear. Mom would make us breakfast (usually oatmeal or a heaping bowl of Lucky Charms), get our backpacks ready, and tell the two of us to get in the car. We'd hop in the back seat next to one another, eagerly awaiting the fate of our morning. I always held my breath a bit for this part, as I knew the history of this car. Mom seemed nervous too, wondering if we would make it to school on time, or if we would be late again. She would look in the back seat at Tom and me, and we would simultaneously count to three and say all together, "START MAGIC CAR," as if we had the power to start that thing up. It worked. Usually . . . on the sixth or seventh try.

When Dad wasn't working, he liked to frequent a local drinking establishment down the road from where 'the shop' was. Usually after work, he would go there for a beer with my grandpa to celebrate another long, hard workday. One beer would turn to two, which would turn to three . . . and soon, the bar became his 'home away from home.'

My dad's always been a bit of an opportunist in a way. Back then, he liked to have his cake and eat it too. If there's one thing I've come to learn, though, it's that you can't sit at both tables, if you know what I mean. You see at this point, my dad still looked like the Marlboro Man, and that went over pretty well with the ladies at the local tavern. I don't ever remember Mom questioning him on this, though, or yelling at him. She had a silent anger about it. One that you could feel so words weren't necessary. She just took the hand she was dealt and did her best to work with it. Truth be told, I was convinced growing up that we were just a blue-collar family with blue-collar problems. As it would turn out, not every blue-collar family was like this. In fact, quite the contrary.

On more nights than I can count, Mom would have dinner on the table, and there would be one empty spot where Dad was supposed to sit. She would try to keep a cheerful demeanor, but the empty seat would stare you dead in the eyes as if taunting you not to look away. As young as I was, I still knew something was wrong. Just like the Bronco, she would try to turn dinner into something fun. After seeing the disappointment in Tom's and my little faces, she would say, "You know what?! Let's go to the store. You two can pick out any TV dinner you want." Of course, we'd always pick the ones with the best treat. That was fun for a while, but while you can easily fix broken cars, you can't easily fix broken homes.

Mom would always forgive Dad. She accepted people and situations for who and what they were. When it came to my dad staying out late, she made it work. She'd invite Aunt Mary over to visit and help with us. When it came to the Bronco, she also made it work. She would eventually walk Tom and me to school, and to her part-time waitressing job that was several blocks away. In hindsight, she caved too soon. Even when she would put Tom and me on time-outs, she would give in and let us out before the time-out was even over. Perhaps her heart was just too big, or perhaps she didn't want to destroy the only real home she was trying to build for herself.

One winter night when Tom and I were in first grade, Mom, Tom, and I were finishing eating our TV dinners, watching the *TGIF* lineup, when suddenly the TV abruptly shut off and the house went pitch-black. This was the first time this had ever happened before. Tom and I looked over at each other for answers and then Mom for some reassurance. Everyone was still for quite some time. Mom then quickly got up, walked towards the kitchen calmly, and began searching the junk drawer for some kind of candle or flashlight to bring us light.

Tom and I, still in the dark living room, heard her softly crying by herself in the kitchen. Looking back, I believe these are the moments when kids start to lose their innocence. I know it made me start to question things. I also wish I could go back to those moments of struggle and hug her, and tell her she's doing a pretty damn good job.

Mom somehow managed to find a flashlight, get us into bed, and reassure us that everything would be 'just fine.' She even said before putting us to sleep, "Playing in the dark can be fun. Yeah, *together* we can make it fun." Later that evening, though, when Dad got home, I heard my parents arguing downstairs about Dad forgetting to pay the electric bill. It's not that they didn't have the money, his priorities were just on different things, so he forgot. It was never talked about again, and the next day the lights were turned back on and it was like it never happened.

Like most things, my parents' relationship was complex. It wasn't just missing dinner and not paying the bills. It was a deep pull towards one another too. One night, Mom was downstairs folding mounds of clean laundry, watching a show, and eating pumpkin seeds, her favorite snack, with Tom and me sitting beside her. The pink silk nightgown she was wearing had a huge rip in the side of it, but she wore it a lot as they were her favorite pajamas. Dad, smirking, came up behind her and playfully told her he would rip them off if she didn't throw them away and let him buy her a new pair. Mom got up and tried to walk around him, but before you knew it, they were running through the house, laughing until tears streamed down both of their faces as Dad tried to catch Mom.

He eventually caught up with her and did just as he said, ripping them even more. By this time, they were rolling on the carpet like two teenagers in love, laughing, hugging, and kissing. Tom and I watched the whole thing. I remember in that exact moment thinking I would never settle for any relationship that didn't resemble that kind of *playful, fun love.* Even through the bad choices, they were best friends. It truly was a one-of-a-kind bond. Back then, I thought our lives and my parents' marriage was perfect. It wasn't until I was much older that I realized, while their love had potential, it also had flaws, and our lives were far from perfect.

IN-LAWS

Mom eagerly announced, one random weeknight, that she wanted to host a family dinner at our house with her great-grandparents (her maternal grandparents), and her mother (my grandmother). She proclaimed aloud to my dad that she wanted her side of the family to see our home and visit with 'the twins,' as her grandparents hadn't yet met us before. As I understand it, we were their first great-grandchildren, and that meant we were already special to them. At least *bragging rights* for sure. It was to be a nice sit-down spaghetti dinner with all of us on our *best* behavior (less pressure for Tom and me as we were still very young). Dad was to step it up.

Mom demanded that the house be in tip-top shape, which was unusual. Ever since I can remember she believed a house should look lived-in (Dad was always the neat one, walking around cleaning up everything in sight). Dad reluctantly agreed to the dinner, as formal sit-down meals were not his kind of thing. However, he knew it was important to Mom, so he was all in. The table was beautifully set with our best fine china, the meal was hot, and Mom was ready.

My great-grandfather, from what others have said, was very successful in a well-to-do, self-made kind of way. He was hardworking and the chairman of a couple of highly successful companies (one of which was a large publication company). My great-grandmother was soft-spoken, poised, and quite lovely. The two of them were composed and well-respected. This side of my family was also very Irish. My grandmother always liked to add little Irish traditions into family holidays to remind us of our heritage. She also loved St. Patrick's Day and never missed an opportunity to tell us grandkids who St. Patrick was (a Christian missionary known as the 'Apostle of Ireland' who converted thousands of Irish people to Catholicism). Later in life, Tom even had a shamrock tattooed on his chest to proudly display his family roots.

Unfortunately, that same tattoo would later become relevant in the most horrible way.

Anyway, back to the dinner. Mom requested that the house stay spotless during this dinner endeavor and all of us dress nicely. While she was in the kitchen cooking, Dad shouted to her, "So Liz, what do you need me to do for this dinner?!" Mom replied, "Whatever you do, Gary, just don't mess up the house!" Ten minutes or so before the guests were about to arrive, Dad decided it would be a good idea to let the dog out. He opened the back door of the house, not realizing the fence was also unlocked and wide open. The dog barged right past him, trampled through the vegetable garden, and ran straight out the fence into the back alley. Dodger was our first family pet, and he was always getting into some kind of trouble. As he ran through Dad's legs and out the door, he also took with him a vine he had ripped out of the garden with around twelve cucumbers hanging off of it (now trailing behind him). Dad had been waiting patiently all summer to pick those cucumbers and eat them when they were just perfectly ripe. Dodger was now dragging them as he ran down the alley. Dad was pissed.

He ran outside after the dog and continued to chase Dodger in hopes of getting him back in the house and calming the chaos before our important dinner guests arrived. Dodger would let my dad get within a foot or so of him, and as soon as he would reach out an arm to grab him, he would take off running again. This happened around five or six times, leaving Dad gasping for breath and infuriated. After around ten minutes of this epic chase, Dad threw his hands up in the air and walked back towards the front door shaking his head. He was now at the front of the house, as he had chased Dodger all the way around the block. Dad figured he'd go back inside, thinking maybe the dog had returned home during the chase and that Mom had let him in. He also assumed he had some more time to locate him, as there were no cars parked out in front of the house yet.

Dad swung the front door open and hollered up the stairs thinking that maybe Mom was upstairs freshening up. "Liz, this stupid, mother f---ing dog is an as*hole! For the life of me, he won't let me catch him! I chased him all the way around the block! Let him run away! I'm completely out of breath. Of all days to run away, he WOULD pick this one!" he shouted. Dad's 'shop talk' was now coming out in full force. "Oh, and by the way, he ruined all of my f---ing cucumbers! ALL OF THEM! JERK! I'M LETTING HIM GO! HE CAN FIND HIS OWN WAY BACK! DAMMIT!" No one answered from upstairs. No one answered him at all. Complete silence.

Dad then turned his head towards the dining room where

everyone (including our guests) were now gathered around the table having small talk. They had parked in the back alley, so Dad hadn't seen their car when walking in the house. My grandma was astonished. In fact, Dad told me she turned a little white in the face. Dad was mortified. Silence took over the whole room for what seemed like the longest minute of his life. Then my great-grandpa let out a big chuckle, which then turned into roaring laughter. Soon everyone at the table was laughing. As Dad was explaining the story of what happened, a neighbor knocked on the door holding Dodger by the collar. At some point during that dinner, Dad told me that my great-grandpa leaned in towards him and said quietly, "Gary, we're all human. It's okay. Please don't feel bad. Also, that is a GREAT story to tell later on!" And he did.

Dad always had an emotional authenticity about him that demanded a liking to him. Even when you wanted to be mad at him for something, you'd end up forgiving him. He's that person you *want* to be mad at, you *are* mad at, and then you forget *why* you're even mad. I always found this trait to be annoying and endearing at the exact same time.

TOMMY

"Geronimooooooooo!" Tom yelled while throwing another matchbox car down the heat register into the basement where my dad found a new project to work on: building Tom and me a new play space. I watched Tom as he pelted that thing down as quickly as he could. I didn't know if this was something we could get in trouble for or not, but per usual I let Tom take the lead. This went on for days, with Tom throwing different objects down the heat register where Dad was intensely working.

One Saturday morning, while Dad was in his 'play space building zone,' Tom chucked another matchbox car down the chute as hard as he could into the basement. We both had an ear towards the chute listening for the *big drop*. That car pinged loudly all the way down until it hit the cement floor. Within a few minutes, we heard, "Tooooommmm" in a strange voice echoing back up the laundry chute. We whipped our heads towards each other, confused as to whose voice it was. It sure didn't sound like Dad's. It was deeper and more profound. It sounded a bit baritone even. "Tom," the voice said again. "This is God. Quit throwing cars down the laundry chute." Tom's mouth hit the floor as he looked back over at me with wide, saucer-like eyes and ran down the stairs as fast as he could to tell Mom that God himself had spoken to him.

Mom smirked, rolled her eyes, and yelled downstairs for Dad to knock it off. Tom and I then walked downstairs together to see Dad's latest creation. Our four total, twin eyes were AMAZED! What stood out the most were the walls of this space. They were shaped like an octagon. It was truly a masterpiece, and it was special because it was our VERY own shared little room with lots of toys and beautiful new carpet. It took Dad several weeks to complete this project, but once complete, it was perfect! We loved playing down there because while Tom and I had separate bedrooms, this was one space we could share and play in together. The Frame Avenue kids liked it too, because it gave us all privacy to play away from our parents. What was new and exciting for us was new and exciting for them too.

This little downstairs gem also gave Tom and me privacy away from our many babysitters. Looking back, I'm pretty convinced that Tom and I went through more babysitters than all the kids in our grade school combined. My parents had a *very* challenging time finding and keeping them. Tom would come up with these elaborate plans to sabotage sitters and get them off the rotating babysitter roster. One particular incident involved this new play space and some 'fresh meat.'

My parents were out on a date and hired a new babysitter to come watch us so they could have a night out on the town. Most of their 'nights out on the town' consisted of them going to either the bar my dad would frequent or the restaurant where my mom waitressed. We always knew which one they went to because the next day, Tom and I would be given a 'beef stick' from Dad's favorite bar or dessert from Mom's work.

While Tom and I were downstairs playing, he came up with an idea to lock the new babysitter in the basement after suggesting she come look at our new play space. He planned to call her down and have the two of us run past her back upstairs as fast as we could and shut and lock the door.

"Sam," he called from the play space. "Come on down and check out what our dad built for us." "Oh no," I thought. "This is *not* going to be good." Sam came downstairs with an overly optimistic attitude and a huge grin of excitement on her face. I feel like her immense optimism just made this plan that much worse. As soon as she got downstairs, Tom quickly grabbed my hand and we went running back up the stairs as fast as we could, where Tom slammed shut the door behind us and locked it. She knocked several times, politely asking to come out, but Tom looked at me, shaking his head, letting me know not to let her out.

Sam knocked for quite some time. She started out politely asking us to let her out, and then I'm pretty sure, as the banging got louder, I heard a slew of profanities come out of her mouth. To be honest, that was the first time I had ever heard the f-word. As soon as Tom decided to let her out, she called our parents right away and told them to come home immediately. My parents flew home, and when they walked in the door, the babysitter announced loudly, "I QUIT!" and slammed the front door behind her.

That was the only time I ever got spanked in my whole life. I have never seen my parents more upset than they were that night. Some of it, I'm sure, was that their date ended early. The other part was they lost another babysitter. I know you're probably thinking that Tom was a little shit. The truth is, he was sometimes, but he was charming and funny too. He had character, and a lot of it! Just like Dad.

For our birthdays, Mom would always take us individually to the grocery store to pick out a special treat or present for the other one to bring to school the next day. One year, Tom picked out a teddy bear wrapped at the bottom of a Happy Birthday balloon. He brought it to school and convinced his teacher to let him come into my classroom and sing to me. His teacher thought this was a great idea, and his whole class lined up around my classroom watching and snickering as Tom sang "Happy Birthday" to me in his popular Elvis voice. He then got down on one knee and handed me the teddy bear and balloon with his arms stretched out wide for a hug. He stared at me with the biggest smile on his face like he was proud to share the day with me.

I blushed so hard that day, but deep down I loved it, and I loved him. I wished I could be as confident and funny as him. I promptly handed him the birthday balloon I had picked out for him and gave him a quick hug back then shrunk back into my desk seat. Our teachers then looked at each other and smiled as if they had just reunited long-lost siblings. It's a feeling you can't explain to others, but twins have a connection. A deep, soul connection that can never be broken. After all, we did inhabit the womb together, and while we were fraternal twins, we just 'got each other' in a way that can't be explained. Even when one dies, part of their soul lives on in the other. I'm pretty sure when one dies, you inhabit some of their traits just to survive.

CHURCH STAIRS

Dad would usually wake us up early on Saturday mornings for long driving excursions around the city. Mom sat shotgun, and Tom and me in the back seat. The windows were rolled down, '80s hair was a-flyin', and music was blasting loudly as Dad pointed out all the work he had done around town. Tom and I could feel the base of the music rumbling from under our small butts in the back seat. We would all listen intently as Dad shouted over the music the backstory of each and every concrete job that he and Grandpa did or were working on. Typically, a slight synopsis would come with each. A city contract they outbid, a big job for the school district, a job for a prominent last name in town, or just a unique project they worked on together.

During these excursions, we would listen to every great musician who ever inhabited the earth. That is one thing about my parents, they had *excellent* taste in music. For our family, music was happiness. It was connection. And Stevie Nicks, that fearless, fucking queen, was always a fan favorite.

There was one set of church stairs we would routinely

frequent, as my dad was particularly impressed with this job. Concrete Placement Company had a heater installed in those stairs that melted the snow and ice to keep the churchgoers safe. Mom, Tom, and I all knew the ending to this story, and that the heat would melt the ice to keep everyone safe, but we let Dad revel in his glory and all acted as though we had never heard or seen it before. "That's really cool, Gary," Mom would say. Tom and I snickered in the back seat.

After the long morning drive, Dad would then usually start a project around the house, or we would end up in one of the neighbors' backyards. You could usually catch me by Courtney or Mya. We would play and the parents would socialize with an adult beverage or two in hand. If we didn't end up in a neighbor's backyard, we would at least see each other on *the block*. Many of the neighbors would be doing yard work, and some would just sit on lawn chairs out in the sun watching their kiddos play. There was such an innocence about that time. It was also the late '80s, early '90s, so parents were more lax with their parenting style back then. This made things fun.

All the memes you see about it today are pretty much true. We played outside. We climbed trees, rode bikes together, made up songs, put on plays, had lemonade stands, built forts, hung out on playsets, you get the idea. We had no internet, no cell phones, and our parents could only find us by yelling our names loudly out the front door or by asking a neighbor if they had seen us. No one hovered over us, and when we scraped a knee or fell off a bike, we got ourselves back up, dusted ourselves off, and tried again.

I even remember Mom giving freeze pops out to all the neighborhood kids too. She'd stick her head out the front door on hot days and yell for Tom and me to come home. She'd have a handful of colorful freeze pops in her hand (with the tops already cut off), and then give them to us to hand out to all the neighborhood kids. During my childhood, this was how parents kept their kids hydrated in the summer. That and Kool-Aid. This is also how Tom and I felt 'cool.' We'd sprint back to our friends, showing off the freeze pops, ready to give them out one by one to the neighborhood kids. There was a playfulness about this moment in time.

There was laughter, fun, bare feet, barbecues, '80s cut-off jean shorts, flip-flops, green grass, yards that had pride behind them, good friends, music, and so much love. Times were simple. We could walk or ride our bikes anywhere on the block, and our parents could trust that we would be okay. We'd be looked after. You could truly count on your neighbors, as they were some of your best friends.

Frame Avenue wasn't just a street we grew up on. It was safe. It was home. It was a place of endless potential. I still drive down that street and reminisce. Our hearts were rooted on this street. It was a great place to grow up, and it was the start of a lot of beautiful memories that are forever in my heart. Unfortunately, though, for me, things didn't stay this beautiful forever. I've learned nothing ever can, and life is always ebbing and flowing. Most of the time we have no control over it because life is a fine balance between empowering ourselves and remembering that we really have no real power at all.

HE'S MOVING OUT

Tom's and my day started out like any other weekday. Mom woke us up, we got dressed, ate breakfast, and rode our bikes to school with the neighborhood kids to attend our careers in the second grade. After school, we hopped on our bikes and raced our friends back home, then slammed our bikes down on the front lawn as if declaring victory. We then ran inside the front door and threw our backpacks down in a rebellious way too. Up until this point, it was an uneventful day. Things felt ordinary, until we got inside to ask our mom for an after-school snack.

Now something was different. You could feel it in the air. There was a staleness. A different energy permeated throughout the house. Something unfamiliar. An elephant. The look on Mom's face confirmed this. She stared at us with a look I had never seen before, and tears welled up in her eyes. She looked scared, like this was the moment she knew she would break our hearts forever. Dad was standing next to her. They asked us to sit on the living room couch together because they had something to tell us. We each sat down on one end. "We're separating," they said. Tom and I peeked over at each other, unsure of how to respond to this. "Your dad is going to be moving out. He's going to take Chance too," Mom said. She then told us that he would be staying at the "shop" until he could get settled somewhere permanently.

"Do you two have any questions for us?" she asked. The only thing I remember I wanted to ask was where Dad was going to sleep. The shop office didn't have a bed. It only had one brown leather reclining chair tucked in a corner, a fax machine, a couple of pictures, a red-and-white clock which read 'Bob's Clock,' and a desk. I was also upset that we wouldn't be able to see Chance every day, especially when we needed him the most. He was our comfort and companion. He was supposed to be there for us through the hard times. "No," I said.

I felt like I took a sucker punch straight to the stomach. Like the life I had once known was blown up right in front of me, and I was watching the pieces fall all over the floor, never to be put together the same again. Like a puzzle that now had missing pieces so could never be quite right.

A divorce is a divorce, but if you believe that one event can change the path of many lives, you will eventually see the devastation this day had on all of us. I've often thought of my parents' divorce throughout my life and wondered, "Had they stayed together, would Mom and Tom still be here? Would my life have been easier?" I've pondered the idea of the butterfly effect. The notion that the world is deeply interconnected, and one small occurrence can influence a much larger complex system. My parents' divorce was the occurrence. The losses, heartache, grief, and pain I would experience afterward were the *complex system.*

It felt like the rug was ripped out rapidly from underneath

me (unfortunately, a feeling I would become all too familiar with in my life). Tom and I, only eight at the time, couldn't grasp the long-term effect this would have on us or our lives, or what the next few months would look like for us.

The truth is, though, even when we were told this, I did not think this would end up a permanent thing. I mean my parents *really* were in love. I know every kid wants to think that about their parents, but you could tell mine were by the way they looked at each other and how playful they always were. I just couldn't wrap my head around the idea that two people could be in love and not be together. That is not how it happens in the movies. The characters lock eyes, fall in love, and everything works out. They live happily ever after. The end.

Unfortunately, I would come to learn in my later years that you *can* be in love with someone and not end up together. For many different reasons, they don't have to make any sense at all.

I don't exactly remember the day my dad officially moved out of the house. He didn't take all of his belongings or make a big, dramatic exit. I'm pretty sure he didn't think this was a permanent arrangement either. Remember, my mom had a long history of forgiving people, and my dad had a long history of using his humor and charm to win her back. He even bought us a gerbil, brought it to the house one day, and got on one knee to present it and its elaborately decorated cage to Tom and me with tears streaming down his weary face. This was his way of apologizing and trying to impress Mom. Tom and I excitedly took the cage and walked it over to Mom to show her. The look on her face said it all. She didn't even have to speak. She didn't budge this time. Things felt different. They were stale, old, rusty, and played out. She finally decided to put herself first. Dad's nightly bar stops were too much. She was done, and she wasn't turning back. Anyway, I think something was wrong with that gerbil because, despite us feeding it, it eventually ate its own tail.

The next few months were *really* hard. It felt like the lights had gone out in the house again. This time not from forgetting to pay the electric bill, but because all the love, lightheartedness, and fun was sucked out of the air. Mom did her best to keep us all going. We went through all the motions. Tom and I went to school, she went to work at her waitressing job, and she even found us a therapist to talk to about all the changes in our lives and their inevitable, eventual divorce. Her positivity, love for us, and belief that this was the right thing to do held us all afloat.

Tom and I also became closer during this time because we understood each other's pain and what a broken family now felt like. The other thing I remember very vividly was that Mom had an extra boost of confidence. You could see it in her face and the way she walked. I couldn't understand why this was until I was much older. At the time, it bothered me. I was actually a little hurt about it. Why didn't we feel how she felt?! In hindsight, I think it was the first time in her life that she wasn't reliant on a man. Didn't need one, didn't want one. She was determined to rise above the adversity and be the best mom and person that she could be. She even enrolled in a computer class at a local community college. This was *big* for her. That took courage, and she wanted to be brave and pave a new path for herself.

After their separation, we stayed on Frame Ave. a little while longer. Thankfully, since we relied on the 'Frame Avenue Crew' to keep us all afloat. Playing with my friends on the block was the only thing that made me feel somewhat *normal*. Eventually, both of my parents ended up in their apartments on opposite ends of town. Mom was awarded full custody of us, and we were to see Dad only on the weekends. Mom's two-bedroom apartment was down the street from our elementary school. She thought it was ideal because not only could we stay at the same school, but she could walk Tom and me to and from school every day. Tom got a bedroom, I got a bedroom, and she slept on the couch every night. This place had a pretty tiny, ugly kitchen too from my recollection, and quick meals became even more popular. She didn't mind, though. She had her fresh start.

Dad's apartment was about ten minutes away from Mom's on the other side of town. We liked going to his apartment because it had a balcony that Tom and I loved to play on, and his apartment unit was tucked in the back of the building by a small wooded area where we could explore. We would escape there, play for a few hours, and make up different lives for ourselves. Dad also let us watch HBO and eat whatever we wanted. I remember Tom and me staying up late to watch *Tales from the Crypt*. Tom would also force himself to stay up a little later than me in hopes of seeing a boob or two on late-night TV. We both made a pact not to tell Mom.

Eventually, we met another set of twins (girls) who lived directly above Dad's apartment. We started out talking to them from below before we could even see their faces. They were only voices from above at that time, but we were amused. Eventually, one day we climbed up to meet them. I can't remember their names, but they were identical and loved talking about soccer with us. We even kicked the ball around with them sometimes, and they showed us a few cool tricks like hitting the ball with our head. After a while, if we weren't climbing up to their balcony, they were climbing down to ours to knock lightly on the patio door (as if using their own Morse code) to ask us to come hang out. I don't even think Dad knew we were up there sometimes. He was depressed that Mom had left him, and was hiding in his own world at this time.

I remember my grandma stopping by once to bring him a box of silverware, pictures, salt and pepper shakers, towels, a *pep talk*, and other knickknacks to help furnish his new apartment, and try to lift his spirits a bit. It was a no-go. It was a nice attempt, but it didn't work. He continued to mope. I remember he also told us that if Mom dated anyone, to please never say their name around him. He made sure we knew that he didn't want to hear about it.

I was embarrassed about their divorce. Parents *were* getting divorced back then, but the rate in the early '90s was lower than it is today. Most of the kids in my class had parents that were still together, and because of this I always felt *very* ashamed inside. This made me hide behind Tommy even more. I pretended sometimes that he was my shield. At one point, my teachers wanted to do specialized testing on me, as my anxiety was SO high that it was affecting my academic performance. I was clamming up inside, particularly during tests, and therefore would score very low, even when I knew the answers. I know I knew because I actually studied. They finally encouraged my mom to let them do testing on me outside of the classroom to make sure I didn't have a learning disability. I don't remember what they concluded, but I do know I got extra time on tests and was sometimes asked to answer test questions verbally versus writing them down. Something about that must have stuck with me to this day because I still get *very* anxious at the word *test* or *result*. My hands clam up, my heart starts racing, I sweat, and I automatically feel like I'm going to faint.

I also remember very vividly that within a year or so of their separation, our third-grade teacher, Mrs. Stillman, called me up to the front board to help work through a simple math problem. I was absolutely terrified. All the other students were sitting on the 'magic carpet' watching me, and I remember my heart felt like it was going to explode. I walked up to the front of the class and looked out into what felt like a stadium full of eyes on me. I couldn't even make out the faces of people; they all looked like blurry shadows. Our teacher was such a sweet lady with no ill intent at all. She was actually one of mine and Tom's favorite teachers, and the only teacher we ever had together. I think our school did that purposely, looking back, since our parents had just split. My teacher held a smile on her face as if I would nail this equation, but that's not how it played out.

As soon as I got up to the front, I looked at my classmates and was convinced that they could see right through me. All of the changes in my life came flashing through my mind, and I felt like my whole class could see directly through the hole in my heart. I instantly started balling. Ugly crying. The type of crying you only want to do at home, alone. I was holding so much inside of me back then, and I felt exposed and completely naked. After my mini elementary public meltdown, Mrs. Stillman hugged me and told me to go sit back down next to Tommy on the rug. "Thank God!" I thought. She never called me up again that year.

CHANGES

After the divorce, we not only had to move out of our childhood home, but we also had to deal with our parents 'seeing' new people. They didn't settle in with new people right away, so there was a slew of oddballs we had to initially meet and put up with for short periods before they both settled down permanently. Fortunately for me, Tom had a sense of humor that made the beginning part of this phase a terrifically funny one. Just like our babysitters, Tom made sure there was a hazing phase to see who would stick around for the long haul. He wasn't opposed to bribing anybody either. He'd go for the cheap shot if he had to. He wanted to turn this divorce calamity into a funny one for both of us, and he did. His goal was to see what these *newbies* would do for *us*.

Dad dated more people than Mom did. Shortly after their divorce, he started seeing a lady who, thanks to Tom, had a present for us every time we saw her. I don't recall her name, but the first time we were introduced, Tom challenged her to a staredown as he took one sip of his orange soda at a time to see if she would crack. Eyes locked, he glared at her through his thick, brown-framed glasses for several minutes without blinking. His lips pursed as if to say, "Don't eff with us." He wanted her to know that he wasn't going to make this easy on her. He didn't.

After a slight hazing phase, we got all the latest toys and gadgets on the kids' market. Never anything too expensive, but due to the ongoing gifts, the fact that she had multiple cable channels, and that she always ordered all the pay-per-view boxing matches on important 'fight nights' so Dad, Tom, and I could all watch together, she earned Tom's approval pretty quickly. She also had a pretty cool brown Lab that Dad took pheasant hunting with him a time or two. As for me, I was quietly waiting and watching. Toys didn't impress me, cable didn't impress me, and late bedtimes didn't impress me. I just wanted consistency. She didn't last long.

Mom only dated two people after my parents separated, or at least that I knew about. She moved in and became engaged with the second one rather quickly. So much for her independent phase. Looking back, I think she caved too soon again. She was just gaining her beautiful butterfly wings of independence, and, in my mind, she went right back to being a cozy caterpillar. She chose safety and security because she thought it was the right thing to do for the three of us.

I can't blame her. I just wish I could go back in time to that moment and tell her that if she just kept making herself happy, we would all eventually be *okay*. She did what she thought in her heart was right, though. Soon we moved into our future stepdad's home, and she was married to him less than two years after my parents' divorce. It was quite an adjustment, to say the least.

They got engaged on their first Christmas morning together.

I remember it like it was yesterday. Mom was holding her steaming cup of coffee, sitting comfortably on a velvet brown chair (furniture that was thoughtfully placed in the home that my future stepdad previously lived in with his ex-wife). He leaned over and handed Mom a beautifully wrapped box with a bow on top and mouthed to her quietly to open it. She daintily opened it, starting at the ends, trying to avoid tearing the wrapping paper. Once opened, she pulled out a beautiful long, red peacoat with black buttons down the front. She then held it up and displayed it for all to see. He grinned and then told her to try it on. She did.

I remember glancing over at her and seeing tears streaming down her face as she pulled a small black ring box from the coat pocket. Tom and I quickly jerked our heads toward each other, impatiently waiting for what was next. She slowly opened the box, turned it around proudly for all to see, then smiled and nodded her head yes. "SHIT!" I thought in my ten-year-old head. My heart dropped into my stomach like a ten-pound paperweight, but I forced a fake smile on my face for her. I had a lot of feelings that day. Maybe, like most divorced kids, I had silently hoped that my parents would eventually get back together and live happily ever after. That dream was now indefinitely crushed into a gazillion small bits on this snowy Christmas morning. The Christmas music softly playing in the background now seemed to be mocking me. Laughing right in my face. Something changed in me that day. I instantly felt older.

We also gained a new stepbrother and stepsister, but Tom and I actually considered our new stepsiblings friends. It was a fun phase, and fortunately (for the most part) we all got along pretty well. People were always comparing our blended family to the Brady Bunch. Our neighbors, people at school, pretty much everybody. That was the go-to reference for all of us. Our stepbrother was two years younger than Tom and me, and our stepsister was the same age. Sometimes it felt like us older ones were triplets.

Right from the start, Mom instantly became an amazing mom to them too. She stepped right up to the plate and never skipped a beat. Truth be told, this was hard for me at times because I had to adjust to not being my mom's 'only little girl' anymore. I was also scared that Tom liked my stepsister more than me some days. Sometimes I felt shoved to the side. There were days that I wanted Mom and Tom all to myself again like the 'Three Musketeers' we once were. I know that might seem like a selfish thing to say, but that's what I was used to, and again, I just wanted consistency.

The four of us kids could always be found playing outside somewhere on the block. We played Power Rangers, put on plays, made up fake movies and recorded them with a video camera, rode bikes around the neighborhood, and played kickball, kick the can, and ghost in the graveyard with the other neighborhood kids. We shot hoops in the back alley, and one of my personal favorites: riding our bikes around the neighborhood with baseball cards in our bike spokes pretending they were motorcycles. My stepsiblings came up with that idea, and Tom and I were amused by it. We were always taking turns using our imaginations and figuring out creative things to do.

Truly, we didn't watch much TV aside from Saturday morning cartoons. My new stepsister and I even made a pretend office in the basement and called it "The Question Company." We had pads of paper, Post-it notes, pens, and even a corded dial phone that was unplugged (so we could make imaginary phone calls).

We pretended that we had just started a multimillion-dollar company that we were the head honchos of. The idea behind the company was that it could research and answer any difficult question one had. We basically just wanted to write things on sticky notes and place them all over the desk to feel important. Of course, there were a few hiccups here and there, but for the most part (for a blended family), it worked. All the fun entertainment we were having with our new stepsiblings helped soften the blow of our parents' divorce. At the very least, it kept us distracted.

APPROVAL

Dad wasn't a fan of our new family arrangement. His heart ached, and he longed for my mom, and he wanted his family back. Although I recognized it was his actions that led to the divorce, it still pained me to see him suffer. Every Sunday night when he dropped us back off at our new home, with our new family, I could tell it crushed his soul just a little bit more. I internally felt conflicted. Should I be happy or should I be sad? I remember staying awake at night and feeling 'sorry' for him. I would toss and turn in my bed thinking about every little detail of the weekend spent with him. They usually ended with him driving Tom and me to the store and letting us pick out anything we wanted for around the twenty-dollar mark.

One Sunday, I picked out a huge, soft, yellow pillow pal. She had brown yarn for hair wrapped neatly into two pigtails with little blue bows proportionally placed on each side. She also had big teary eyes embroidered onto her face. Maybe back then I related to her because she looked how I felt. I slept with her every night. She was my comfort for quite some time.

I always wanted to tell my dad about all the new adventures Tom and I had with our now stepfamily. How much fun we were having in this new 'honeymoon phase' everyone was in, but I didn't want to turn his dull aching heart into a sharply pained one. So I just kept things to myself. Dad continued to date around and hang out at the bars with his friends. He was now in his mid-thirties, and I think he just wanted to keep busy to keep his mind off of Mom and his mistakes. He wanted to forget (even temporarily) that he lost his family, family home, and family dog, who had to be re-homed shortly after the divorce.

I used to ride my bike to the bar Dad frequented. I knew he'd be there every Monday night for unlimited crab legs, and it was also near his apartment. Sometimes I would knock on the front window outside of the bar, smiling and waving so he could see me, and other times I would quickly ride past, stare into the window to see what he was doing and who he was with, and ride straight back home. At times I would pedal so fast, I'd struggle to even catch my breath. I'd then toss my bike down in the backyard so it looked like I had never left. I never told Mom or anyone where I was. It was my secret.

Looking back, that was the start of me vying for someone else's attention. That was the start of a little girl who was hurting inside and didn't want to feel unnoticed anymore. I think our new family and my parents' divorce made me feel like I had been knocked down a few pegs, and I was still trying to figure out where I fit in with all the new arrangements. When it was just Tom and me, we *were* my parents' world, and things revolved around the two of us. When our family became 'blended,' it felt like someone rearranged a puzzle, and we were trying to figure out how all the pieces fit back together.

I started to become a perfectionist. I remember there was a coloring contest at the gas station Mom always stopped at for gas and coffee. One day, she brought home four coloring pages and encouraged us all to submit to it. She said once we were finished, she would bring them back and turn them in to the front clerk. I colored in the lines the best I could. I took my time, even meticulously tracing around the outside of every part of the picture in bold so that I was sure to stay in all the lines. I even went back to it again after finishing it to make sure it was perfect.

The other kids in my family also colored pictures for this contest, but not like I did. They rushed through it, handed them back to Mom, and forgot all about it. I wanted to win more than them. I prayed to God *every* night that I would win this contest. I didn't even know what I was going to win, but I knew I wanted to. Finally, one day Mom picked me up from school (about a week or so after I submitted my picture), and told me I had won. She said they were going to hang my colored picture up at the front of the store with a Polaroid they would take of me right next to it. I didn't even care about the silly, insignificant prize; I only cared that I had *won*. That mine was the best.

Sometimes we do things to gain the approval of others without even realizing it. We let others and their opinions become more important than our own, and in doing so we actually lose ourselves. I think we've all done at least one thing in life to earn the approval of someone else, and we continue to do this until we heal ourselves. Until we find our voice and muster up the courage to forge our own path, a path that speaks directly to our own heart. I think you truly start to find healing when you live life the way *you* want to and the opinions of others become quieter or are no longer heard.

Here are some things I've done in my life, when older, where I had to earn the acceptance of others: pledged a sorority in college; aspired to be a successful TV news anchor; interned at prominent TV and radio stations; hosted a college radio show (that my dad loved listening to and would park his truck in just the right spot in his alley so he could pick up the station); modeled in fashion shows, hair shows, and a couple of magazines; made a couple of background appearances in popular TV shows (in hopes of landing something bigger); took acting classes at the urging of my modeling agency; and dyed my hair just the right shade of brown because they thought it suited me better than blonde (it didn't). I dated a slew of frogs instead of princes, if you will, because I put my feelings *last*. I learned early on in my life to be a people pleaser, and to put the opinions of others before myself. I learned that I had to work to be accepted, and I learned to stay quiet and work from the outside in, instead of the inside out. In essence, I learned that in order to be loved, I had to be *good*. I also had to stay polite and be quiet.

Make no mistake, I always cherished and loved these dreams. They were mine. They manifested in my own heart. If I could relive all of these moments, though, I would live them for me and only me. I would let that hurt, insecure little girl go. Bid her farewell. I would listen to my inner self, believe in myself (even when others didn't), and speak up for myself in the moments when I needed to the most. I would also remember that the times we are always our most authentic selves are when we are connected to something *bigger*—being a case manager for many years (that was always authentically me, needing no acceptance), teaching yoga, helping others heal (authentically me), writing my story (me). I can't go back, but I can continue to heal myself from the inside out to find authenticity, find my voice, and leave MY mark. I'll do it for me, my mother, and my daughter. I owe it to us.

I can't blame my parents for their separation, and I don't blame my dad for his choices back then. He just did the best he knew how. I've come to learn, now that I'm a mother myself, that our parents only do the best they can. The best they were taught. If they have unhealed trauma from their past, unfortunately, they pass it on to their children without even realizing it. They both had trauma, but they tried their hardest to make beautiful memories for us and hold things together as long as they could. They tried to stay together for us and create a soft landing when things didn't work out as planned. Unfortunately, I don't think they could have ever anticipated what was coming next.

Dad eventually settled down, but it took some time. He dated one person for several years, Eileen, who I still consider my family. They didn't go the long haul together, but we've stayed in contact ever since. At the time, the two of them lived on one side of the duplex that my grandparents owned. By all accounts, my dad and Eileen did a lot of fun things together. I remember them traveling and going on fun adventures, like snorkeling in Mexico and visiting Eileen's costume-designer cousin in Hollywood.

Eileen also tried her best to be there for Tom and me. She drove us to and from our part-time jobs, drove Tom door-to-door to help him finish his paper route in record time, cooked amazing meals for us, dropped our lunches off at school when we forgot them, took us shopping for new clothes so we could stay trendy in high school (which seemed very important at that time), and drove our friends and us to the movies or any other places we wanted to go. She even attempted to teach me how to drive a stick shift until I accidentally smashed her car into the garage. I remember walking into Mom's house, her eyes wide open, as Tom answered the house phone, "Oh, you're looking for Amy. She'll have to call you right back. She just crashed a car into the garage."

She even had a way of convincing my dad to give me money so that I could go to the mall and keep up with my wardrobe (which now seems so incidental, but back then was at the top of my priorities). Eileen and I had a mutual respect/love for Sheryl Crow. We'd jam out to her CD in the car on the way to the mall as loudly as we could, singing every word at the top of our lungs. She tried to get along with my mom too. They even shared books together, as they were both avid readers. When one was done with a good book, they would pass it on to the other one to read as well. Then they would talk about the book like their own small, private book club. I even started staying by Dad's (outside of just the weekends) because I actually enjoyed being there during this time. It was lighthearted and fun, and I felt safe and loved. The house was colorful and full of plants, and authentic art, and smelled good too. There was also always something delightful cooking in the oven, and the aroma would fill the whole house, which now had an eclectic feel to it.

Despite all of this, Mom wasn't exactly thrilled about the situation (just like Dad wasn't when Mom settled down). It became obvious, as time went on, that my parents never really fell out of love with each other. By this time, it had been about seven years since their divorce. They both had become complacent, settling into their separate lives. Mom was becoming particularly unhappy during this time. I overheard her telling a friend on the phone once that she was having horrible flashbacks of her child-hood triggered by smells, sounds, songs, etc. She then noticed me listening and closed her bedroom door. She was also sleeping a lot more than usual. On top of all of this, she was silently struggling with fibromyalgia. I'm not sure if her depression exacerbated her fibromyalgia or the other way around. She didn't talk about it with us much, but I know she was in pain (both physically and mentally).

One afternoon, while I intently watched her put on her makeup, she told me, "Amy, whatever you do in this life, don't settle. Make yourself happy, and the rest will always fall into place. If you don't do that and you settle and take the easy route, life will be *very* hard." She then opened her lipstick and meticulously put it on, as she then admitted to me that her heart still skipped a beat when Dad walked into a room. I was in my early teens at the time and did not know what to do with this kind of grown-up information. I was just trying to see how to put on makeup and be near my mom. I never forgot her words, though.

I think my parents questioned if they maybe had thrown in the towel too soon. Maybe they both loved each other, but still had some growing to do. After all, they met young. When Dad would come over to pick up or drop Tom and me off, my parents would end up in the den talking for hours. I'm not sure where my stepdad was at the time, but he and Mom had started to grow more and more distant. At times, Mom would even sleep on the couch.

Sometimes, I'd catch my parents flirting. Mom would smile and flip or twirl her hair, as Dad made her laugh like old times. She would shuffle her feet, looking down and smiling, or shove him playfully on his shoulder as they cracked inside jokes and talked about us, 'their twins.' This soon became the norm, which I liked—Mom had a spark when she was back in Dad's presence. Also, they were getting along and co-parenting well for the two of us. I felt good about this, until one cold winter night in January when I was at Dad's, and I was woken up to the worst news of my life. Mom had died.

MY FIRST BIG LOSS

After Mom passed away, I was left with a huge hole in my heart. I struggled immensely. This was a really painful time, and I cried a lot. I felt really scared, and hope seemed harder to find. People say everything happens for a reason, but I just kept searching for the reason. "Why me? Why her? What did we do to deserve this?"

To be more like Tom, I started smoking Marlboro Lights and even a Marlboro Red here and there ("cowboy killers," as Tom called them). I also started drinking beer on the weekends to numb the pain. I even skipped school with my best friend whose mom had also died, just a year prior. We'd vent to each other and talk about how much life *sucked*. We talked about how irritating it was when our other friends complained about their moms in such frivolous ways when we had to go through the roughest years without ours. Most of their complaints seemed irrelevant, or like things we'd *want* to complain about. Like "Oh, your mom won't take you to get your belly button pierced this weekend?" Seemed incidental when our moms were dead.

Sometimes we'd even drive through fast food restaurants

and eat our feelings in the parking lot while listening to sappy songs. Then I'd light a cigarette and blow the smoke out the window nonchalantly along with the rest of my feelings. We found it amusing that no one would ever know we ate all the junk food we did since we both had a fast metabolism at the time. There's no rule book on grief, so in our developing teenage minds, these coping skills worked. Most high schoolers don't want to talk about death and grief that much, as it's considered *depressing*. So we decided we'd just be depressed together.

Mom died in January, which was the same month as mine and Tom's birthday. Nineteen days before our seventeenth birthday, to be exact. Our family always made a really big deal out of each other's birthdays, especially my mom. This year, we didn't feel like celebrating. I remember we were both sitting in the living room watching TV in silence. Tom was on one end of the couch and me on the other. A sitcom was playing, but neither one of us was laughing. It seemed a bit ironic. When Dad finally returned home from work around five, he handed us each a gift bag with tissue paper in it. We both got the same black pair of Adidas track pants, size medium. We thanked Dad, but when he left the room, I cried. Tom hugged me.

I felt a void. A huge void. I just missed her. Every day, I missed her. Mom had hopes, she had dreams, fantasies, desires, heartbreaks, wishes to see the world, doubts, questions she needed answers to, traumas to be healed, and more. She had more to give, more to see, and more to learn, but she couldn't. Life didn't give her the chance. She died young. She was forty-three years old when she died, just five years older than I am now. That's hard for me to comprehend sometimes. It used to seem old, but now it seems young.

We didn't learn about it until later on, but Mom died of an

allergic reaction. She had taken a pain pill and an allergy pill simultaneously and gotten sick while she was sleeping. She fell asleep on the couch that night and aspirated in her sleep. From my understanding, my stepbrother heard her coughing and the dog barking and found her. He immediately went and got my stepdad, and the paramedics were called right away. While they were able to resuscitate her, the damage to her body was already done.

If I could go back, I would hug her. I would ask her what was wrong. I would understand the deeper meaning behind her physical and emotional pain, and I would sit right by her side. I would scratch *her* back, play with *her* hair, and make *her* favorite meal. I would hold *her* hand. I would listen. The relationship between mother and daughter changes in the most beautiful way when we grow older, and I would give anything to see that relationship now. Sometimes I daydream about it, and what it would look like. I imagine how she would be as a grandma, and how she would have loved my daughter the way she loved me. I remember her goofiness and her smile, the way she smelled, the way she brushed her hair, and her hands. I remember her hands and her perfectly manicured nails so vividly. Then I smile and hold my daydream close to my heart.

For a long time, I just stuck to the narrative that we were told. That Mom's heart had stopped working. It was easier and less painful to say out loud or think about. It also struck less of a reaction out of people because it sounded less complicated and sad. I'm not upset with the adults in our lives for telling us that. I see why they did. I really do. It turns out, though, they may have discredited her beautiful heart. A heart that made my mom the amazing soul she was. It also turns out that someone *else* was blessed with that same, beautiful heart. And for that, I'm truly grateful.

HE HAS HER HEART

My mom was an organ donor. As it would turn out, while Mom was hooked up to life support, the doctors were able to keep her organs healthy enough to donate to recipients in need. She died on January 5th, 2002, and on January 6th, 2002, someone received my mother's heart. While doing research and looking through an old box of photographs, I came across a letter written by a man who stated that he was the recipient of my mother's heart. He continued the letter with some background information about himself and his family, and he expressed his sincerest gratitude for the second chance he was given at life. A life that was given to him because of my mother. He shared that because of receiving her heart, he's been able to see his daughters get married, and the birth of his grandchildren. Since then, he's also lived an extra twenty-two years and counting.

When I read the letter, I felt different feelings. Mostly awe and disbelief. It was truly heartwarming for me and restored my faith. After doing a bit of research (and with the help of some friends), I was able to locate the man. He lives within twenty minutes or so from me. I was shocked to find that he not only lives in the same state, but he lives close by. I eventually found his phone number, and finally, after an hour or so, built up the courage to call and introduce myself to him. Even though my heart was pounding and my voice was shaky, I decided to make the call anyway. I introduced myself and let him know I found the letter. He was gracious and kind, so I felt at ease. He listened as I told him about the beautiful person my mother was.

He said he'd always wondered more about whose heart he had. He said that he has always been grateful and that he likes to joke with people and tell them his 'heart's' age because it is younger than his actual age. When he told me that, I simultaneously laughed and cried. He said he had always wondered if anyone had received the letter he'd written twenty years ago. He was unsure all these years, and he's happy to know it's been received. He also told me that he's always known he's had a special heart, but now it's been confirmed.

Hearing that my mother's heart saved someone else was *very* healing to me in many ways. Especially since we were originally told it had stopped working, and that it had died when she died. It's healing to know that the best, most beautiful part of my mother was passed on to someone else.

Because of her loss and the important lessons she taught me, whenever I feel like giving up, I don't. I hold on for my mom. I push myself harder because I'm taking her with me. I'm taking her just a little bit further than she got to go. Taking her to experience all the things that she didn't get to experience. I'm working on healing traumas that she didn't get to heal. And in the hard moments, the moments when I feel like giving up but don't, those are the moments that I feel her presence the most.

Waukesha author surprising discovery 20 years after her mom's death, her heart lives on

Article and photo from Milwaukee's TMJ4, May 31, 2024

AUNTIE MARY

After Mama passed away, Auntie Mary stepped right up to the plate to help Tom and me in any and all ways that she could. Maybe we couldn't ride our big wheels across the street to her house anymore, but she would drive the twenty minutes or so into town to our dad's *anytime* that we needed her for something. Now that I'm a mother myself, I can't even begin to express my gratitude to her for holding us up during this hard time. We were absolutely crushed inside, and she was a constant for us in our time of need. She became a second mom in a way, a comfort, just like she was when she lived by us on Frame Avenue. Her smile, her soothing voice, her consistent optimism no matter what the situation, and her ability to turn any defeated situation into a pragmatic one. She always found a solution. No matter what. She was the bright light in our dark.

She once told me (later in life), that while Mom was in the hospital hooked up to machines, she made a promise to her to always be there for Tom and me. She walked into that sterile hospital room all by herself, held my mom's hand, and told her the plan she had to watch after us. Told her that she would do the best she could to pick up the pieces where my mom had left off. She promised to always make sure that we were safe and well taken care of, and she stepped right up to the challenge.

She knew that she could never replace our mom (her sister), nor did she want to, but Auntie Mary did have a very maternal instinct that kicked in the day after Mom died. Since she never ended up having children of her own, she always told me that I felt like the daughter she never had. She said that she felt like her sister had left her a gift. So there she was being an AMAZING sister to my mom, even when Mom had left this earthly world for good. Auntie Mary was also never a person to go half-in on anything. Everyone who knew her knew she was all in, or nothing at all. And she was all in on being there for Tom and me.

She helped us get our driver's licenses (which must have been scary as hell), helped us with difficult homework (she was a schoolteacher, so homework was always a top priority), drove us around town to apply for part-time jobs, showed us how to properly fill out job applications (to get said jobs), took us shopping when we needed something, and listened to every single teenage problem we were going through without passing judgment. She also helped me through the first of a series of teenage heartbreaks, as she was the only person in my life that I trusted with that stuff at the time (aside from my mom, who was no longer here to offer advice and wipe my tears away).

Auntie Mary picked up the phone day or night to listen to me cry when I missed my mom. Sometimes she'd cry with me. One weekend I even saw her pull up in the back alley of my dad's house and get out of her car, struggling to carry a huge box up to the patio door. I was sitting on the patio table outside, and I remember thinking to myself, "What the hell is she carrying?!" I jumped up and helped her get it inside and up the stairs to my bedroom. She had bought a computer for me. I had mentioned over the phone one day that it would be helpful for schoolwork during my senior year of high school, as I was enrolled in a typing class at the time. She remembered I had said that and went out and bought me one. She even set it up (along with a printer she got too).

Her goal was to set us up for success. She taught me to want more for myself and my life. She taught me that I didn't have to just accept and settle for the cards that I was dealt. That I could force a new hand. That I could question things. Having that new computer was also incidentally when I discovered my love for writing, which she avidly encouraged as well. I began to journal about my loss every day, and the new and difficult feelings that came along with it. In fact, she was the first person who ever read something that I wrote. I accidentally left a creative writing assignment in the front seat of her car when I ran inside to grab something at my dad's one day. When I got back into the car, her eyes were wide with excitement, and she was smiling from ear to ear as she praised me for my 'beautiful writing.' She then went on to tell me that I had a talent that I shouldn't ignore. I laughed and shook my head when she told me this, but she didn't. She was serious.

Even though Tom and I were still living with Dad, he really wasn't home that much. He was working a lot since he still had the concrete business to run. I also think, looking back, that he was *trying* to stay busy. I'm pretty sure that he was grieving the loss of my mother too, but he didn't know how to talk about it

or what to say to us. He didn't know what to do with that kind
of messy, emotional, unexpected grief. It started to become more
and more evident that anytime Dad was hurting or upset, he just
went to work. It was *his* safe place. The familiar thing that he
knew best. He'd keep his mind busy by going to the shop, cleaning the house until there was nothing left to clean anymore,
or finding more projects to do. Anything that involved physical
movement, as the pain was just too much for him to sit with.

Dad and Eileen eventually ended their relationship. Dad
admitted to us that he tried his hardest to make it work for
Tom and me because he didn't want us to lose any more people
in our lives. He also said he stayed longer than he should have.
Eventually, though, he couldn't hold on anymore. They were just
two very different people. He said he was trying to create stability for us, but if I'm speaking God's honest truth, it started to
become anything but. After several years with Eileen, she eventually moved out. Dad settled into another relationship *very*
quickly. She was someone he had already been friends with and
had known for years. He told me one day that he had actually
liked her for a while, but was scared to pursue anything because
of Tom and me and all the changes that we had already endured.

Eventually, they ended up together and had two more children (my younger half brothers). They are quite a bit younger
than Tom and me, but they mean the world to me to this day.
I think because they were so much younger, I also became very
protective of them. I loved them both SO much from the moment they were born. I even helped change diapers, played with
them, babysat them, and taught them new things. I remember
Tom even taught the older of the two how to tie his shoes. He
was very proud of that. They were a true joy for us, but Dad's

time was now occupied even *more*. That was hard for us back then. Between his new family, projects, and running a business, there really wasn't much time left for Tom and me, who were still thick in the grieving process.

Throughout our late teens and early twenties, Tom and I leaned heavily on each other and Auntie Mary to get us through. I also became very close with my older cousin, Matt. He became like another brother to me. His lighthearted, goofy personality seemed like a necessity at the time. A breath of fresh air. Matt's also never been a person to overthink things, which I always viewed as a strength. I wished I was more like that since I've always tended to overanalyze everything for as long as I can remember.

Matt is just an uncomplicated person. He shows up exactly who he is. We were always playing stupid pranks on each other, going rollerblading, sharing music and burning new CDs, and hanging out on the weekends with each other and each other's friends. A true friendship blossomed. He'd even grocery shop and make big, elaborate meals for Tom and me at Dad's when he was done working. He too worked for the family business, so he would head over after he was done with work. Anyway, we didn't know how to cook, so we appreciated this skill of Matt's. It made us happy and helped us forget about our pain for a bit. I remember Tom, Matt, and me standing in the kitchen joking around and waiting for good food.

Matt also saved us from Dad's go-to meal, which was canned peas and corn atop a piece of white bread, served up slightly soggy. The canned vegetables atop the bread would cause the bread to become soggy, and would sometimes even create a hole in the bread's center that would cause the vegetables to fall through the bread base when you tried to pick it up to eat it. I don't like peas to this day because of it. I also don't like TV dinners, boxed meals, chicken potpies, or milk (since we were always encouraged to drink a large glass of it with every meal, even if we didn't want to). Anyways, Matt's meals were a little more of what Mom used to cook for us (before our parents separated), and that we appreciated. It brought back a little nostalgia.

During this time, Tom really began to *struggle*. Some days I could tell he was barely holding on. Prior to losing Mom, he dabbled in smoking weed and partying here and there. After her death, though, it became clear that he was really trying to numb his pain. This was absolutely heartbreaking for me to witness, as I felt like I was slowly losing my brother now too. Tom just wasn't exactly sure where he belonged anymore. Where *we* fit in. We had both lost our mother, our stepfamily, and now Eileen, and we were struggling to adjust to a new life. A life that really didn't make much sense to us anymore.

Mom was always our anchor. When we looked around at our new surroundings, in our new life, the only thing we recognized was each other! He tried to stay in the 'big brother' role I had delegated to him after Mom died. Eventually, though, the roles reversed and I became the *big* sister . . . for good. I became the one who was always watching out for him. After all, he was my twin, my other half. It was his time of need, so I let him lean on me, and I became the protective one.

Tom's personality really started to change. I witnessed him go from outgoing and funny to isolated and mean. When Tom was struggling or dabbling in harder drugs, he'd hide. His confidence would take a big hit. He knew what he was doing wasn't right, and he'd choose not to be around anybody (even me, his best friend). I remember his face would always break out too, leaving his shame exposed for the whole world to see. We started to go down different paths as he began experimenting more and more with drugs.

Auntie Mary and Dad both tried to intervene and help Tommy. Dad even tried motivating him by buying him a car and using it as an incentive to 'straighten up.' It worked until Tom got the car. He was smart like that; he knew how to play the game. He also knew how to find free resources when he needed them. One time he even called me from our local hospital's emergency waiting room because he didn't have a cell phone and he knew it was free. I thought it was an emergency until I picked up and Tom started a casual conversation with me.

"Tom, where are you?!" I asked.

"I'm up at the hospital. Phones are free to use here, and they also have good food."

I couldn't believe it. Sometimes I think Tom was too smart for his own good. He got 'bored' easily, and it was hard for him to stay focused for a long period of time. This made it harder for him to accomplish his goals.

Dad pulled out all the stops and even tried having a couple of deep, heartfelt talks with Tom to let him know how *loved* he was. I was sitting by Tom on the other end of the couch for one of them. It was the second time I had ever seen my dad cry (the first being after my parents divorced). Expressing deep sentiment out loud wasn't exactly Dad's forte back then, but he really gave it all he had for this particular talk.

He told Tom that he was his first son and that he loved him deeply. That he may not have always been the best dad, or done all the right things, but he tried the best he knew how. The best that *he* was taught. That every day when he was at work, he would worry about him. That he would think about him from the moment he woke up to the moment he laid his head on his pillow and try to come up with solutions to help him. That he was sorry for everything that Tom had to go through (including his mistakes), and that he loved him very much and only wanted him to succeed.

He said that he missed our mom too. That she was a friend to him (his best friend growing up) and that he loved her too. That he was doing the best he knew how, and that he wanted to do better, to be better. I'm not sure how much Tom cared about Dad's sentiment at the time, but I cried. I think I even pretended that some parts of Dad's talk were for me. After all, I was hurting too, I just responded differently to the hurt than Tom did. I knew if he acted out, I had to be 'the good one.' That didn't mean that I didn't want to act out, though. I think I would have acted out more if Tom had not, but I wanted to protect him, so I stayed on the straight and narrow.

Eventually, I graduated from high school while Tom was working towards his GED. He had gotten kicked out of high school for skipping out too much, so he went to a local community college to finish his GED. This time in my life is painful for me to talk about because twins already have an obstacle to face from birth. Something they didn't sign up for but gets assigned to them anyway. Every twin knows that they are innately going to be compared to the other during their lifetime (if not by their parents, then their peers). This was always hard for Tom. His twin sister was now graduating from high school and being celebrated for this accomplishment, but he was not.

While it pained Tom deeply, it also made me feel guilty for my success, as I wanted to share it with him. We even had a couple of our senior pictures taken together in the beginning of our senior year (per Auntie Mary's request and hope that Tom could still pull it together and graduate). I even remember that Tom demanded that we take at least one standing up because he was 'finally taller than his sister' and he wanted to show it off to the world. The senior pictures that Tom took were never published, though. I'm pretty sure his spot in the senior yearbook said 'not present.'

Sometimes I would stare at Tom's smile and try to believe it, try and convince myself that it was real, but his smile always looked cracked for some reason. I can't explain it. It just looked like it wasn't authentic. Like he was forcing it, and his pain was becoming too great to hide anymore. The loss of Mom hit him hard. They had a bond. She always saw the good in him no matter what, and that trauma affected him deep in his soul. Recently, our family played some home movies we had filmed from early Christmases, and I saw Tom and that same smile. It hurt my heart for a whole day. I lay in bed and couldn't stop thinking about it.

Thankfully, Tom still had his sense of humor, though. No matter what life threw at him, his humor was still there. Like him knocking on the patio door (to get my attention) and mooning my first boyfriend and me when my boyfriend leaned in for a first kiss.

I remember we were standing in the back alley of Dad's house after a memorable dinner date. We were staring into each other's eyes, my heart pounding with excitement, as I knew what was coming. My boyfriend (we'll call him "A") started to lean in for a first kiss. "Here it comes," I thought, "our very first kiss! Eek!" Just then we both heard a loud knock, followed by more knocking.

We turned our heads in the direction of where it was coming from only to see a bare ass pressed up against the patio door. "Who's that?" A asked.

"Who's what?" I asked, pretending I hadn't seen the full, pale moon proudly on display for us both to view (my face now completely red with embarrassment). "Oh, the butt you mean?!"

Now A looked completely confused as if butts were just regularly on display at our house.

"Oh, that's just my twin brother, Tom."

I was *absolutely* mortified until A burst out laughing. Then Tom turned around and smiled while waving a beauty pageant-esque wave topped off with a little wink at the end.

That was Tom's way of being protective (to stop the kiss) and make us smile at the same time. We both just shook our heads laughing. Humor was always how he coped. He made others laugh, even when he was lost and hurting deeply. That was his superpower, and it remained even through his darkness.

WHITEWATER

After high school, Auntie Mary helped me apply to colleges. I was a little reluctant to go because it felt like I was leaving Tom behind. I really wanted to go, though. We finally decided that I would go to a two-year college (around town), and then I would transfer to a four-year university after that. I attended community college and lived with my dad for a little while longer (after graduation) while I worked for my grandmother's magazine company. It worked out nicely, since my grandmother's condo was just down the street from my dad's house, and school was only a couple blocks in the other direction. I did this for my first couple of semesters, but eventually I moved out.

In the summer after my eighteenth birthday, I moved in with my cousin Matt. He had a two-bedroom apartment and was looking for a roommate. I was so excited the day he called up at my dad's and asked me to move in with him. Some of my high school friends even helped me pack up my belongings and move. They were thrilled because I was one of the first people in our group to get a taste of freedom from having my own place, and this meant they were going to have some freedom too. Dad did not want me to move out. He begged me to stay just a little bit longer, but I couldn't wait to have my own place.

Matt's apartment was about twelve minutes from Dad's. It was an older building with a peculiar smell and a strangely strict landlord (who, as it would turn out, was also my parents' landlord from their very first apartment together). I asked my dad several times if they had paid their rent on time, as she was never really that friendly to Matt and me from the get-go, but he reassured me, "Every month." Anyway, we had a pretty sweet apartment unit. Each of us had our own *wing*, so to speak. My bedroom and bathroom were on one side, Matt's on the other, with the living room, dining room, and kitchen in the middle connecting them both.

Our dining room table was actually a poker table on one side that could be flipped back to a regular table on the other. On the weekends, it would get flipped to the poker/party side, and by Monday, it would get flipped back around to the eating side (like the crazy, fun weekend with our friends never even happened).

We had a blast there. Our friends were over a lot, and it was just an exciting time. Matt was going to school and working, and I was too. He ended up dating a couple of my friends, and I kissed a couple of his friends. They were older than me by a few years, and this felt rebellious (something I was never really able to be before). I also knew it annoyed him a lot when they talked about his 'cute little cousin,' so I have to admit that this made it even more fun.

Tom found an apartment at this time too, along with a support group to help him stay sober. He discovered a gym that he liked to frequent, got a long-term girlfriend, and he even managed to get his GED. He also decided back then that he wanted to go back to school to become a personal trainer. It felt like he had come out on the other side. Like we both had. I felt relieved. I had my brother back.

After I completed two years at community college, I transferred to a four-year university to get my journalism degree. UW–Whitewater was around forty-five minutes away from my hometown. This was the perfect distance to feel like I was independent, yet close enough to drive back home when I needed to. Auntie Mary's house also wasn't too far for me either and was on the way to school. Sometimes I'd drive there on weekends to do laundry and spend time with her. I'd also drive home frequently to check on *all* of my brothers.

I lived in Whitewater with three other girls in an old, rickety yellow house with a cool screened-in front porch just to the left of some old railroad tracks. My best friend, Anna, and I transferred there at the same time from other schools. We were excited because we now got to live together and experience college life together. We even went and picked out different shades of pink to paint our new bedrooms. The pink was a terrible idea, but we didn't care. We were thrilled about our new adventure.

Another one of our high school friends also transferred there at the same time as us. Soon, we all started to hang out together. I loved college life, and I finally felt like I could escape from the hardships of my past life for a little while. I pledged to a sorority (where I met new friends and held the social exchange chair), anchored for the college TV news station, hosted my own radio show, joined a couple of organizations related to my advertising minor, and developed *many* new friendships. I also started working as a caregiver for adults with disabilities at a local group home there. This was my favorite job, as I finally felt like I was making a difference in the world. The only problem was I couldn't cook for anything, but my boss at the time was teaching me how.

In a way, college felt like a fresh start for me. A place where I could completely start over. I even started to wear a brainy-looking pair of black-framed glasses everywhere I went. I wore them because they made me feel like someone new. Someone smarter. Someone who came from a different life. A life with an easier past. I could pretend, even just for a little bit, to be someone different. Someone special.

Tom would also come up to Whitewater to visit me regularly. Even though he didn't go to college there, he started to become friends with everyone in town. They all started to know and like my 'funny twin brother.' That wasn't surprising to me. That's who he was. He was easily likable. I liked having him there too, because I could come out of my shell more with him around. Sometimes I'd even take my glasses off and let myself be vulnerable. I also didn't mind him coming to visit because my guilt around us going in different life directions lessened when I felt like he could also experience 'college life' alongside me.

All the fraternities and sororities started to know him too and kept asking me when he was coming back up. He'd go to parties with us and was like the older brother again, making sure my friends and I all got home safely and that no one hit on his 'little sister.' Everyone knew him, everyone liked him. There was just one problem: he started drinking again. I would catch him with a couple of drinks in hand from time to time at the parties. I tried to say something to him about it, but he'd become angry and defensive. He told me he was 'fine,' and that he could handle a couple of beers. He'd say, "If you can, I can." I eventually stopped saying anything about it because I knew if I did, I would push him away, and I didn't want to do that. I wanted him by my side.

During college, I started to see a school counselor to talk about the pain I harbored from losing my mom and the other childhood dysfunctions I had endured. I really liked this counselor, and I knew I had to start talking to someone to begin healing. During 'Bring Your Mother to the Sorority' day, it hit me incredibly hard that I was *never* going to see my mom again. That she wasn't going to be there for any of the important milestones like Mother's Day, birthdays, college graduation, my wedding, and even when I had babies. Even though Auntie Mary came to the sorority house that day, I remember feeling so depressed after the event. I recall looking around at all my sorority sisters laughing lightheartedly with their moms as they served them breakfast, and I was holding back tears the *entire* time. My heart felt like it was going to explode.

That was a pain that hit deep, and talking to this counselor in college really helped me to process things and normalize my pain. I saw her for many, many months. I remember her even discharging me from therapy, letting me know I was doing quite well and to come back whenever I needed to. Ironically, the timing of her words was the week before my *second big loss.*

THE DAY EVERYTHING CHANGED

Tom told me on the phone one Saturday that he was coming up to Whitewater to help me touch up the paint on my all-pink bedroom. I waited patiently for him to drive up that morning, and even set aside some pictures that I needed him to hang for me too. I was really looking forward to us painting and spending the day together. I waited and waited until I finally saw his black, noisy car pull up. When he walked into my bedroom (where I was waiting), I remember thinking how nice he looked. He was tall and muscular like Dad used to be at his age.

At that point, he was going to the gym a lot, so he had transformed into a bigger, more muscular version of his prior self. He was dressed nicely in a button-down flannel and jeans (also like my dad), and his smile was actually genuine. It didn't look like it hurt him to smile; it was sincere. He even greeted me with a big hug and then proceeded to tell me that the Easter Egg pink color I chose to paint my whole room was *ugly as hell*. We both burst out laughing.

That day, while Tom and I were painting together, I asked

him if he remembered my favorite Christmas as a family. "Hey, Tom?" I asked. "Do you remember that Christmas where Mom and Dad blasted Fleetwood Mac and we decorated the tree together in our matching boy/girl robes?"

He grinned. "Yeah, of course I remember. It was *my* favorite Christmas," he said.

"Mine too," I said. I tilted my chin in his direction and asked, "Why was it your favorite Christmas?"

He stopped what he was doing, looked back at me straight-faced, and said, "Because we were all together and happy. Life was simpler. There was hope," he said.

I teared up a little and told him that I agreed with him. I also reminded him that we still had Chance (our dog) at that time too.

We both then reminisced about Chance and our childhood years. I couldn't believe that he not only remembered that day but that it was his favorite Christmas too. Then, and I'm not sure whose idea this was, we blasted Fleetwood Mac on my old CD player, grabbed hands, and spun each other in circles like we did on that Christmas years before.

I remember the room becoming a huge pink blur behind Tommy, as he became the focal point as we spun each other in circles until the point of dizziness. He was now all I could see as we laughed together so much it hurt. We then both fell to the floor on our backs, staring around at the ugly pink room and laughing until tears streamed down our faces. The sun beamed on us through the bedroom window. It felt warm and was shining on us like a spotlight. Like we were the only ones in the world who existed that day. I hadn't laughed like that in forever. He then helped me touch up the paint, hang up some pictures, and we reminisced about our past and about how fun Frame Avenue was. It was one of the best days I had in a long time. A day that would also become one of my favorite *memories*.

On April 7th, 2007, I was working a shift at the group home I worked at in Whitewater, incessantly attempting to reach my brother. He had been up to visit me the night before to watch a movie and eat miniature, pre-packaged cherry pies that he had saved in the trunk of his car. When he went down to get them the night before, I laughed because only Tom would carry minia-ture pies in his trunk to bring out at just the right moment. They were delicious. We ate them and watched the movie *Where the Heart Is* together. We sat on opposite ends of my couch with my feet going in one direction and his going in the other (like we al-ways sat when we were younger). It was a great night, but I hadn't heard from him since he left the following morning. I remember trying not to panic that Saturday, but everything in me felt like something was wrong. Like something was *terribly* wrong.

I had just made and served dinner to all the residents at the group home, passed their medications, and was starting to get ready to help them with their bedtime routines when I caught a glance at the news station that was airing on the living room TV. It was usually playing softly in the background, as it was one of the only channels the group home picked up. I also watched the news a lot, as I was going to school to be a news reporter and liked to pick up local news tips. I remember thinking that I could have sworn the black car they had just flashed across the screen was my brother's car, but the words that followed next just couldn't be about him. It didn't make sense. "A 22-year-old man was shot this afternoon in Milwaukee. Police are still on the scene, and the investigation is ongoing."

Fight or flight immediately kicked in, and my whole body started trembling. My heart was pounding so loudly that I could actually hear it. My knees became weak, making it hard to walk. I hurried to get all the residents into their bedrooms so they didn't see me panic. Then I grabbed my cell phone and called home immediately. My stepmom answered the phone. I pretended like I wasn't freaking out inside and casually tried to ask what the upcoming Easter plans were again (even though I knew exactly what they were). I calmly tried to ask about them, but the first thing she asked me was where I was. "Oh my god," I thought. "Stay calm, Amy," I said to myself. "Stay calm."

I told her that I was working and asked her, "Why?!" There were long pauses in between our sentences, and that's when I knew and reality started to sink in. That's when my fears started to come to fruition. She told me that I needed to get a ride back to my apartment immediately and that Dad and her were headed to Whitewater to come and get me.

"Why?" I asked.

"Amy, please just work on getting a ride back to your apartment. We will be there shortly," she said.

By this time, I could barely breathe. I remember one of my favorite residents had come out of her bedroom in her robe to see what was going on. She was always so motherly towards me, and I could tell she was really worried about me. Like she just sensed something wasn't okay. She was deaf, so she was signing to me. She mouthed to me from across the room, "Are you okay, Amy?" I nodded my head yes and forced a smile until she believed me and went back into her room. As soon as I heard her bedroom door close, I ran to the kitchen as fast as I could to use the house phone. My hands were shaking so badly as I tried to dial Aunt Mary's phone number that I kept pressing all the wrong buttons.

When I finally reached her, I asked her immediately if Tom was okay.

"Yeah, why?" she asked.

"Are you sure?!" I asked again.

"Yes, Amy. As far as I know, he's just fine." Just then, her other line was beeping in. She asked me to hold on for a second. I waited for what seemed like an hour, and when she clicked back over, I could tell by the tone in her voice that something terrible had happened.

She tried reassuring me that everything was okay, but there was no way in hell I believed her. I knew her better than that. Her voice sounded completely deflated and defeated. I had never heard her sound like that before. I quickly hung up the phone and called my boss, who coincidentally had young boy/girl twins of her own.

"Please get someone to come in NOW. I need to leave work immediately," I told her.

"Why, Amy, is everything okay?!"

I tried explaining to her what I *thought* had happened, but I didn't really know myself, so I'm sure I sounded absolutely crazy. I must have convinced her, though, because she inevitably got the next staff person on duty to come in early to relieve me.

When he came in, I immediately ran past him and hurried towards my roommate's car, which was now waiting for me in the driveway of the group home to take me back to our apartment. I don't even know who called her. Maybe I did, but I don't remember. I just knew she was there waiting for me. It was a clear decision to leave my car since I'd be in no state to drive anytime soon. I was onto something from what I had seen on the news and knew I shouldn't drive. The whole way home was silent.

I stared out the window, praying so hard that what I had seen on the news was somehow NOT about my brother. I then prayed if it was about him, that he survived. That he would recover from whatever he had gone through and be okay. I also thought he would be so mad at himself for not staying with me longer in Whitewater like I had begged him the previous morning to do. When I got back to my apartment, I waited on the balcony, watching over the railing to see my dad's truck lights. When he finally got there, I slowly walked outside and sat in the back of the truck as we started the forty-five-minute drive back home. It was eerily quiet.

"Is Tom okay?" I finally mustered enough courage to ask. "Please tell me that Tom is okay." And yet, when my dad opened his mouth to reply, I screamed, "STOP! GIVE ME A MINUTE. I'M NOT READY!" I knew that the information he was about to tell me was going to change my life and who I was forever.

In that moment, driving with my dad, I could have had a million thoughts. I could have wondered why or how this had happened. I could have thought about my mom, I could have thought about asking my dad to pull over so I could run as far away as I could from all the madness. Instead, one question took the forefront of my mind: "If Tom is dead, am I still a twin?"

I don't know why that was my first thought. My mind was racing in all directions, and my body was literally shaking. I was freezing, but the heat was blasting on me. "Is Tom okay?!" I asked again.

"No," he said. "He's not."

"NOOOOOOOOOOOOOOOOOOO, NO NO NO NO!"
I sobbed. And that's all I remember from that point in Whitewater
until Dad drove me to the hospital. He pulled up to a local hospital back in our hometown and walked me to the front door where
Auntie Mary was waiting for me there too. Auntie Mary and Dad
both hugged me on each side as I screamed and cried. By this
time, they had told me that Tom was killed. I had never felt more
broken before. I had never felt more lost. They carried me through
the hospital door and told the staff what had happened. "Her twin
brother was just murdered," Auntie Mary said, crying. "She's going to need something to help calm her down."

I sat in the emergency room hospital bed and stared off
again at a wall. I then ran to the bathroom and got sick there. I
lay on the cold hospital bathroom floor and remember thinking
that I wanted to be wherever Tom was now. A nurse eventually
came in and handed me two small, blue pills to take. "Please take
these," she said, as she held out her hand. "They're a sedative that
should help you sleep." I grabbed them from her hand and swal-
lowed them so I could be left alone. Then I laid my head back
down on the cold floor and closed my eyes.

Eventually, I was back at my dad's house, where my friends,
family members, and Tom's friends were all there to sit and cry
with me. I don't remember leaving the hospital, or my dad and
aunt taking me back to my dad's. Velette (my roommate) and
Anna (my best friend) drove to see me from Whitewater, along
with a few of my other friends too. I couldn't even tell you who
was all there. Everything was hazy. No one could believe it.

Situations like this one tend to shake you up and make it
hard to see down from up and up from down. The news stations
were continuing to air the story about the shooting, and I didn't

want to hear about it. I didn't want to believe it, and I wanted it to all be over with.

Since they didn't find the person who killed my brother right away, and we didn't know any information about it, the first night was really scary for me. I remember staring out the back alley of my dad's home thinking, "What if I'm next? What if this was targeted? Why Tom?!" I felt an instant obligation to protect my family (especially my younger brothers), but I also wanted to hide. I felt absolutely sick to my stomach. I thought about the idea of the police never finding the person who did this. That thought frightened me to my core. It wasn't until the next day when all the details started to emerge that my family reassured me that I was safe.

It took about twelve hours for the police to find and catch the person who murdered my brother, but they finally did. Every time they flashed my brother's killer on TV, I immediately turned my head away. I didn't want to see him, and I didn't want to learn any of the details. It was way too painful. I was also pissed off because they kept mispronouncing our last name. My brother was murdered, the least you could do is say his name correctly.

I heard later in life that a person witnessed the shooting and was brave enough to come forward. I also heard another witness stayed with my brother, held his hand and prayed while he died. I'm so grateful for these people. They're the true unsung heroes to me, and it's always brought me comfort to know that he was not alone when he died.

A journalist from a local newspaper called my dad's house, asking to speak with me. He wanted to get a statement. At first, I hung up on him. "How dare he call my dad's house asking for me to give him a statement!" I thought. Then I remembered from my journalism classes that if I didn't say anything about Tom, they might keep the story vague (which in my mind would dehumanize him), or worse yet get a statement from someone who didn't know Tom as well as I did. I somehow managed to sit down and focus long enough to write something out. I wrote down all the good things that I could think of about Tommy and who he was as a person. I called the number back and shared what I had written. It was published the next day.

I had called back *for* Tom. I wanted him to be remembered for something other than just a victim. I liked the article. Then, I lay on my dad's couch for days and didn't move. I stayed in the same pajamas, under the same blanket, and slept as much as I could. People came and went with meals, hugs, presents, cards, stories, etc. I thanked them because I knew it was the polite thing to do, but I just wanted my brother back, and unless you could give me that . . . I wanted to be left alone. I didn't care much about anything anymore. I felt completely numb.

I also was stuck on the fact that this wasn't supposed to be how Tom's life ended. He was only *twenty-two*. We were only twenty-two, and he was so full of life yet. I believed that this all had to be a horrible nightmare and that I would wake up from it soon. That I HAD to wake up from it soon. Morning after morning, though, it all began again. The entire tragedy would replay, crushing me as though it was the first time all over again. My life felt *over*.

The thing I couldn't grasp was that not only did I lose him, but someone *took* him from me. It turns out he was killed for a wad of cash he pulled out during the deal. Someone in my family later told me that it was believed to be around three hundred dollars. I can't tell you the amount of times in my life (since learning of that) that I've stared at three hundred dollars in my hand and thought, "This right here is what someone thought my brother's life was worth." How I wish we could've given the murderer that money instead. We'd have given him every single thing we owned.

I still didn't know all the details of his death at the time, but I did know that he was trying to buy drugs. It was a robbery *gone wrong*. He was shot in the arm, which then traveled through his abdomen and pierced several organs, inevitably taking his life. Inevitably then robbing me and our family too. Robbing me of my best friend in the entire world, and the person who knew me the most. The yin to my yang. He was now gone, and I was going to have to somehow process that.

To say that this period in my life was difficult is an understatement. My dreams were crushed, and my strength had been tested to the max. My heart and soul had both been beaten down, leaving me feeling completely *hopeless*. Sometimes it even felt like I was left for *dead*. I could barely move. My hair also started to fall out in handfuls, and I began to lose weight that I wasn't trying to lose.

Somehow, I spoke at Tom's funeral. I don't remember how. I just know I stood up at the podium for about five minutes straight because the words wouldn't come out of my mouth no matter how hard I tried. They just wouldn't come out. A couple of my friends stood beside me to support me, both emotionally and physically holding me up. In a matter of five years, I had lost half of my immediate family, and I started to feel like a wandering, lost soul just trying to find my way home again.

I eventually went and stayed by Auntie Mary's house. I needed a mother's love, and she was the closest thing to a mother I had. She was nurturing and thoughtful, so I decided to take some time off school, stay by her, and just *rest*. I was so tired. Every day I was tired even if I did nothing. People would visit me at my aunt's, but I just wanted to be alone. I just wanted to sleep because then I could visit Tommy in my dreams. It was the *only* place I could see him again, so that's where I wanted to be.

I started to think of all the questions I wanted to ask him. I wanted to know if he was scared before he died, if he was in a lot of pain, why he decided to go and buy drugs when he had found a better life for himself, if he saw Mom, and I wanted to know if he thought about having to leave me when he was dying. That thought alone pained me because I know in those final minutes before he passed (when he tried to drive his car away, but couldn't), he would have been mad at himself for leaving his twin sister behind.

I was angry with him for deciding to use drugs again because ultimately that choice took his life. It was *not* a good choice. He was still a victim, but he put himself in a vulnerable position, and he didn't have to. He shouldn't have. It took me some time to forgive him, but I finally did because we all make mistakes, we're all human, and his mistakes just had unfathomable, permanent consequences.

A couple of weeks after Tom's funeral had passed, Auntie Mary started to give me lists of 'one thing to do per day.' I thought it was stupid at the time. Why is she asking me to get the mail, vacuum the living room, take a short drive, or make myself a sandwich to eat? I was annoyed at her for this. I appreciated her efforts, but it felt like a lot to ask. I respected and trusted her, though, and wanted to continue staying by her, so I did as she asked of me. Every day she would call me while she was teaching (on her breaks) so I could report that I had completed my assigned task. I started to complete them and tell her early on in the day, so I could immediately go lie back down and be left alone.

One day, one of those 'tasks' I saw on the Post-it note sitting on the kitchen counter was 'Take a drive back up to Whitewater and visit with friends.'

"ABSOLUTELY NOT," I told her during our check-in call. "I don't want to drive that far, and I don't care to see my friends or go back to college. EVER! What's the point?!"

I then hung up the phone and went straight back to bed. I pulled the covers completely over me and curled up in my safety nest for the rest of the day, softly listening to Fleetwood Mac songs on repeat so I could fall back asleep. When Auntie Mary got home from work that night, she came up to the room and sat next to me.

"Amy Leigh," she said in her sweet voice. "The point is . . . is that your life is not over. Tom's is. You're still here."

"Yeah, well, I don't want to be," I said abruptly. "I want to be where Tom is."

"You can't," she said. "He's with your mom, and you're here with us. We need you."

"Well, that's not fair!" I said.

"I know," she said. "Unfortunately, Amy Leigh, the hard truth is that life is not fair, and I'm so sorry to have to tell you that."

At twenty-two years old, those words replayed through my head over and over again. My mind processed them as quickly as it could since I had already been searching for answers and a reason why all of this had happened. I realized at that moment that life is completely NOT fair. That things will happen that we have no control over. That we will lose when we desperately want to win, that people can play the game of life with a completely different set of rules than you have, that bad things happen to good people, that just because you want something to happen doesn't mean it will, and that just when you think you have life all figured out, it will knock you straight to your knees to remind you that you're not in charge. And THAT was the moment my childhood magic dissipated and my 'hope glasses' fell off and shattered into a million little pieces.

The old colorful lenses I once saw the world through before would never quite look the same. It was like learning that the Easter Bunny wasn't real. We want to believe it, we do believe it, but once we're told the truth, we can't unlearn it. We can't unsee it. At that moment, all the colors in my world turned to gray. I saw the world for what it truly is sometimes . . . dark. I saw the sad side of the world. The cruel side, the desperate and hopeless one. And I learned that day that life is a game. It's a choice.

Choose to stay down, or choose to get back up.

---

www.gmtoday.com   **LOCAL**

Suspect arrested in shooting of Waukesha man

Waukesha West High School grad remembered as charismatic

By BRIAN HUBER
Freeman Staff

WAUKESHA – A Waukesha West High School graduate was remembered as charismatic Monday, the same day police announced a suspect in his shooting had been arrested.

Milwaukee Police Department spokeswoman Anne E. Schwartz said Monday that an 18-year-old Milwaukee man had been arrested earlier that morning in the shooting. She had no further details on the arrest.

Tom Tegge, 22, was shot while in his car at about 3 p.m. Saturday near North 26th and Center streets in Milwaukee, police said. He was shot in the left arm, and the bullet traveled into his chest, police said this weekend. Despite that, Tegge was able to drive his car for about a block before a collision with another vehicle.

Tegge was pronounced dead at the scene. He was believed to be alone in the vehicle.

Tegge's twin sister, Amy, said her brother "was a charismatic individual with an amazing sense of humor."

"He always loved to make those around him laugh, even if it meant being the brunt of a joke," she said. "Although Tom had to endure many hardships, he always managed to keep his head up high. Tom had a presence about him that would make him unforgettable to those who had the pleasure of meeting him."

For fun, Tegge loved mountain biking, weightlifting, camping and going to movies with his girlfriend of more than two years, Jenny. Amy Tegge said her brother, who was five minutes older than her, held many jobs but his ultimate goal would have been to become a personal trainer.

Amy Tegge said she was working in Whitewater when she saw news on television of the shooting and knew it was her brother, even though he was unidentified, because she recognized his car.

When told a suspect had been arrested, Amy Tegge said, "That makes me feel better."

Tegge, a 2003 graduate of Waukesha West High School, is survived by his father, Gary; stepmother, Tracy Tegge; twin sister, Amy; two brothers; aunt, Mary Baker; grandmother, Dorothy Daganhardt, his girlfriend, other relatives and friends.

(Brian Huber can be reached at bhuber@conleynet.com)

THE CHOICE

I got back up. I didn't want to, but I did. I went through my grief the best way my twenty-two-year-old self knew how. Day by day, I just did the best I could. Through all the mistakes, the important choice I made was to take one small step forward when I wanted to take no step at all. The next day, after Auntie Mary's task request and talk with me, I took the drive to Whitewater to see my friends.

The first thing I saw while driving back to school was a group of guys outside on their front lawn playing beer pong. They had their shirts off and were soaking up the sunshine while laughing and enthusiastically high-fiving each other. I think they even chest-bumped. I remember feeling so upset inside. I was angry that the weather was now nice and that I couldn't enjoy it. I also remember thinking to myself, "How can they be outside having fun, loving life, when I feel like shit? How can life keep going like this when my world feels broken? Don't they know my brother was just killed?"

I also was in such a daze that I walked into the house next

door to my friends' house thinking it was theirs. I strolled through the back door and up the stairs only to recognize absolutely no one. It wasn't until one of the girls looked at me with a puzzled look on her face and said, "Can I help you?" that I realized I was in the wrong house. I quickly turned around without saying a word and exited down the back stairs. I then slow-jogged to the house next door to see my friends. The whole way there, I was thinking to myself, "I hope every day won't be like this."

Eventually, I started attending classes again. Slowly, but surely, I went. I now know that was Aunt Mary's plan all along. She was trying to get me back into 'life,' because unfortunately, life doesn't stop moving when we do. Auntie Mary also notified the school about the tragedy and my brother's loss, and they were very supportive. The dean even came to my brother's funeral to represent UW–Whitewater and express the school's sincerest condolences. My sorority sisters mailed me flowers and messages of hope, and my teachers sent cards and emails of prayer and encouragement.

People I hadn't heard from in a long time reached out. Even our old elementary school teachers all signed a card that included a sweet picture of them with Tom when he was a waiter for their table a couple years back. I saved that picture. He looked so proud.

All my teachers told me to take my time and come back whenever I felt ready. That they would all do their best to help me catch back up and accommodate. Everyone was kind and understanding (which I never took for granted). When I finally did go back to school, I'm sure some of my professors were surprised that I went back so quickly. The truth is, though, I just wanted to feel *normal* again. If normalcy was such a thing anymore.

One professor even said to me while we were walking together in the hallway, "Amy, you're the only person who turned in your assignment on time, and your twin brother was just killed. What does that tell you about YOU?!" He then smiled crookedly and patted my back. "I'm happy to see you back, kiddo. I'm so sorry for your loss," he said. "That's a hard one."

I didn't take the full extensions given to me on my homework assignments, nor did I miss any more full days of school after that. The truth is, it kept my mind busy and off of everything, including the upcoming, pending trial. I also didn't want people to feel sorry for me, or treat me any differently than they did before. Most people in school now knew about Tom's death (and now ALL of my previous hardships), which I didn't like. I never wanted to feel like a victim, so I never acted like one. That's the tricky thing about tragic loss, though; you want compassion, but not too much.

It was still up in the air if there would be a trial for my brother's murder. We had all hoped that there wouldn't be (none of my family had it in us), but we didn't have all the answers yet. We had to be patient and wait. My dad was particularly in no shape for a trial. He was having an extremely hard time with it all, as he was asked to identify Tom's body after the shooting. They were pretty sure it was my brother because of his shamrock tattoo, but apparently, there was some confusion with another person, same name, same tattoo. So Dad had to confirm it was Tom. Truth be told, having to identify Tom knocked my dad straight to his knees, and it was going to be a long time until he could get back up.

Eventually we got the call that there wouldn't be a trial. That the man who killed Tom had confessed to the murder and had

taken a plea deal. I was so relieved when I found out. I still remember standing in the middle of campus when the call came
in and feeling like a huge weight had been lifted off of my shoul-
ders. It didn't bring my brother back, but at least I could *try* to
move forward.

I was encouraged to write and read a victim impact statement at the sentencing if I could. I feel bad about it to this
day, but I just couldn't go. I couldn't face the person who took
my brother from me. The DA tried to convince me, letting me
know that I might regret it someday, but even the thought of
it made me weak. I wrote something, but I left it to my family
to read on my behalf. I begged Tom to forgive me and to give
me a sign that he wasn't mad about me choosing not to attend.
I just knew that if I went to the sentencing, I wouldn't go back
to school. That I would be emotionally drained and need more
time off from life.

One day while talking to my brother out loud in my car (a
week or so before the sentencing), I asked him to give me a sign
that he wouldn't be mad at me if I didn't go. That he could find
it in him to understand that it had all just been too much. First
losing Mom, and now losing him had taken its toll on me. That
I didn't have much fight left in me, and the fight I did have,
I needed to hold onto. That I was already in a really delicate
and vulnerable state just trying to survive, and I needed to save
whatever energy I had left to pick up the pieces of my life. Just
then, a semitruck pulled out in front of my car while driving
that said "Amy" alongside some numbers on the license plate.
It drove in front of me the whole way back to Whitewater. I
followed it right back to school until it finally turned left and
I turned right. I had my answer. I knew that Tom was saying,

"Forget about it. Go and live your life. Live it for us both. I'll always be with you." So, I went back and I didn't give much of my energy to anything else.

My family read my victim impact statement on my behalf. I'm really grateful they did. I'm also thankful for my grandfather who went up to the stand and spoke about his grandson and how much we all loved and missed him. Tom's killer was found guilty of felony murder and sentenced to the maximum sentence of twenty-seven years. In my mind, that wasn't long enough, but I felt like I could at least close that chapter for a little while. I also felt very sad for the defendant's family, as they lost a son senselessly that day too. My heart hurt for his mom's heart, my stomach ached for his mom's loss. My tears fell for *everyone* involved that day. My family AND his family. It wasn't an easy day for anyone. I also tried to find forgiveness in my heart by thinking about Tom and how he would have wanted me to forgive. My mom would have wanted that too. Also, we can't truly move on until we forgive.

After the sentencing, I tried my best to move on. I applied for an internship at a local TV station where I wanted to become a news reporter. I was excited because out of several candidates, I landed the internship. One day, a few weeks into my internship, I got sent on a story where we had to cover a funeral. I didn't know this at the time, or where we were headed. I just hopped in the news van, and off we went. Back then, I was eager to help cover any story I could, and I didn't want to stay at the station if I could be out in the field.

I hadn't shared much about my brother with anyone prior, and I secretly hoped that no one at the station would ever put two and two together with our last names (despite the fact that they covered the story multiple times just months prior). I knew it was in the archives, I just hoped it would never resurface. I was always searching for a fresh start somewhere, and this was another place where I just wanted to leave my hardships at the front door and pave my own path.

Prior to this particular day, I was used to covering light-hearted stories with the morning show anchor. I really liked her. She was funny and well-liked at the station. She took me under her wing right from the start. I even brought her a coffee from time to time as a way of saying thank you to her. She made me feel included and taught me all the ropes and important behind-the-scenes stuff. All the ins and outs of news. Unfortunately, though, she and the photographer couldn't fit me in the van on this particular day.

I was kind of bummed, as they were going to cover a fun story (I believe it was about new animals up for adoption at a local shelter). As soon as I found out there was no room, I quickly hopped in another reporter's van so I didn't end up at the station all day. I didn't know what the story we were covering was about until we were already headed to the location. Turns out, it was a funeral . . . for someone who had been murdered.

The minute I saw we were pulling up to a funeral, I had a complete panic attack in the back of the news van. Hands sweating, heart racing, feeling dizzy kind of panic attack. I tried my best to control it. I took as many deep breaths in the back seat as I could. Once inside, I looked at the coffin ten feet or so in front of me, grabbed the news reporter's hand, and started running. I ran straight out the front door and down the street as fast as my legs would carry me. By then I was crying. Sobbing actually. I finally stopped running when we got to the end of the street.

"Amy, what's wrong?!" she asked. "This is news. This is what we cover sometimes. The hard stuff," she said. "If you want to be a news reporter, unfortunately, you have to be able to handle stories like this. Life can be hard, and this is real life."

Boy, did I ever already know what she was talking about. By the way, this would be the start of many years of being stereotyped as someone who has had it easier. I just shook my head. "I'm sorry," I said as I put my head down and stared at the ground. "I just can't be in there. I can't be on this story right now." I then walked back to the van, sat in back, and waited for her and the photographer to come out. I was so embarrassed and ashamed of myself. I had tried to hide my pain, but I was realizing it was creeping back up when I least expected it.

I finally told her about my brother on the way back to the station, and what had happened to him. I felt like it was the only card I had left to play. The only one left in my hand. I was now almost hyperventilating. I was mortified by the whole thing. I guess my grief was still there, no matter how hard I willed it not to be. Wherever I went, it followed me. It was now my shadow. I now became aware that I HAD to deal with it. There was nothing else but me and my grief facing off with one another.

To make matters even worse, she looked at me before we were almost back to the station and said, "Oh my god, are your parents okay? That wasn't that long ago, less than a year. How are they doing?"

"Okay, I guess," I muttered under my breath. I didn't tell her that my mom was also dead, or that most days my dad was barely hanging on. That I was stopping by his house weekly to make sure he was eating healthy, staying hydrated, and taking his vitamins. That he was going through the motions, but a piece of him died that day with my brother. That the two detectives showing up at his front door to tell him that his son had been murdered was his worst nightmare come true. That I worried about him incessantly, because I didn't want to lose anyone else that I loved. That I had now become the caregiver of my family.

I also didn't want to tell her that every morning around the news table when we all pitched our story ideas, I hoped and prayed that nothing else would come up in my brother's case. That I would hold my breath after I shared my story ideas until everyone else shared theirs. That every story that was pitched (particularly traffic accidents or tragic, live stories) caused me to immediately check in on all of my family members and other important people in my life.

When we got back to the news station, I went straight to my car while she and the photographer walked back inside the station. Before they left, I told them that I was going to take my lunch break. I sat in my car in the parking lot, thinking about leaving the station for good. Thinking about just driving back home and never coming back. Checking out. It sure felt like the safer/easier option. I remembered that I did have choices, and *that* was a choice. I didn't *have* to stay there. I could leave. But something in me told me that I would be okay and to go back in and finish what I started. What I committed to, what I signed up for. That I had to live MY life too. That this grief was something I was going to have to deal with for a long time, and that I could find the strength in me to work through it if I just kept showing up. I was proud of myself for making that choice, and I felt like my mom and Tom would have been too. Honestly, I felt like they were holding me up that day.

I freshened up, fixed my mascara, and walked back into the

station confidently while standing tall. A true 'fake it until you make it' moment. Whether I wanted it to be or not, this was now my story. My reality. I had to own it. I walked straight back to my desk and sat down to do some research for a story I was helping the reporter with earlier in the day. I casually glanced behind me where I could see, through the glass window, the news reporter telling the news director what had happened in the field. Explaining to him why the story may be lacking some serious B-roll.

Fortunately, no one ever said anything more to me about it. I did get a couple extra warm smiles as people walked past my desk. Shortly after my internship was completed, I switched to an internship at a local, popular radio station. We did lighthearted stuff like going to concerts, and events where we promoted the station and handed out free prizes. At least there I didn't have to face the hard realities that had become my life.

THE LETTER

Letter to Tom (read in court at sentencing)
September 27, 2007

I am reading this letter on behalf of Tom's twin sister Amy.

First I would like to start out by telling you about the person whose life was taken away. Thomas James Tegge was an outgoing and friendly guy ever since childhood. He was always pleasant to be around and loved making those around him laugh. Growing up, you could say Tom was a class clown. He enjoyed putting others in a good mood, and when things were difficult for someone else, he used his humor to take their pain away. Tom was in many sports growing up and took a strong interest in soccer, and later on began mountain biking as a hobby. You might ask why I am telling you this. I am telling you this because this is the character of the person that I will no longer get to see every day. This is the character of the person who was loved by so many people, both family and friends. This was the character of a person who did not deserve to get his life taken away at such a young age.

April 7, 2007, is one day that will never be the same to any-one in this family, because on that day everyone who knew and loved Tom was informed that they will no longer be able to see him again. Those who loved Tom are affected by this loss more and more each day as they try to live a life without him. It affects Tom's grandmothers because they will no longer have a grand-son to brag about, they will no longer receive phone calls from him asking them how their day is, or even have a grandson that will offer to help with yard work. It affects Tom's grandfather because he will no longer be able to have long chats with his grandson, and to give him advice about life lessons that he has learned and longs to share.

His loss affects an aunt who was like a mother figure to Tom since his own mother passed away. An individual who guided Tom and loved him the way his own mother would have if she were still here. It affected his girlfriend, who loved Tom and planned on spending her life with him. A person who shared a bond with him and who lost a special friend to laugh and cry with.

It also affects his younger brothers. One who asks about Tom frequently and who doesn't understand or have the mental capac-ity to fathom the crime that took place on April 7th. It affects his other brother who is too young to remember what a great person Tom was, or even the color of Tom's hair or eyes. He will only know from what others tell him. He won't know Tom's laugh, or the way he walked in a room, and neither one of his brothers will have an older brother anymore who would have been able to teach them things that only older brothers can teach.

It affects his stepmom, who has to answer the questions to her son (Tom's brother) about where he went, and if he's okay. Who has to answer other questions like "Mommy, what kinds of things did Tommy like to do for fun? Is Tommy still thinking about us? Did the police go to Amy's house on that day too to tell her that Tommy was gone? Mommy, was Tommy hurt that day?"

Tom's loss greatly affects his father, who is just coming to terms with the fact that he will no longer see his oldest son again. Who can remember teaching his son how to play sports, how to ride a bike, how to tie his shoes. A father who loved his son more than words can say, someone who would have done anything in the world to prevent this from happening. Someone who loved him so much that his son's well-being was the only thing on his mind from the time he started work at 6am to the time he laid his head down to rest.

Lastly, it affected me, his twin sister. Every day I wake up and relive the nightmare of losing my brother in my head. Every day I have to come to terms with the fact that my brother (who was only five minutes older than me) will no longer be here to make me laugh. I have to try and comprehend why in the world someone would do this to another human-being. I have to try and sort through the fact that I lost not only my mother just five years earlier, but now my twin brother from a horrible crime. I have to continue living without the one person in the whole entire world who I loved the most. I have to try and live normally even though deep down inside the pain hurts so much. It hurts so much that some days I can barely breathe. I will be having a typical college day, walking to class, and all of a sudden I remember that my brother, my best friend, is gone, and I have a panic attack right there in the middle of campus. I will be trying to concentrate at work, and it hits me again . . . my brother, my best friend, my childhood buddy, my hero, my class clown, the person I went to movies with, the person I sat by during holidays, the person who I walked to school with, the person I played sports with, the person I told all my secrets to, the person who knew me more than anyone in the entire world . . . is now gone. Just like that because of one bad decision on someone else's behalf. I want all listening to know that I will go on with my life. I will graduate from college, get married, have children, and start a career, but it will never be the same. It will never be the same because I'll look over my shoulder and my twin brother, my best friend, my hero, won't be with me.

GRIEF HAS ITS EFFECTS

When we lose important people in our lives, it will affect us. Grief is love disguised, so when you love someone deeply, you also grieve them deeply. Grief is also not linear. It is ugly. It is hard. It is inconsistent. It sneaks up on you when you least expect it. Grief is two steps forward and three steps back. It is doing things that you normally wouldn't otherwise do. It can turn you inside out, and sometimes it is simply surviving.

The truth is I was not only grieving Tom, but the person I was before his loss, and the trauma of my losses saturated my cells for years to come. Trauma has to go somewhere, and it will stay there until you face it and work through it. When you experience loss, everything around you can become a trigger until you can accept your grief and surrender to it. It can rear its ugly head as panic attacks, lack of sleep, nightmares, body aches, depression, addiction, anxiety, and even hypervigilance. Like seeing something scary on the news and deciding you have to call all your friends and family members to see if they're okay.

You can hear a certain song that reminds you of your lost

loved one, and it can make you want to freeze up and lie in bed the rest of the day. Dating or meeting new people can feel like *hell* because you have to start over with your life story (and relive it all over again). Sleep becomes inconsistent because you might have beautiful dreams of your lost loved one, or you might have bad dreams of them, or dreams of failed attempts of trying to save them. You can even have strange dreams too. I had a lot of flying dreams back then. I know some people associate flying dreams with abuse, but in my dreams, I was just flying to get away. Always just flying away to be somewhere else. Anywhere else. Then I'd wake up and realize I had never flown anywhere. That I was right back to where I started, and the sadness would creep in.

I experienced all of it. The most prevalent for me was anxiety and avoidance. I even remember asking Google, "What happens when you lose a twin? Can you die of a broken heart?! Can a twin survive without their twin?"

I joined an online group called "Twinless Twins." It's kind of a blur as to my communication with the group, but I just wanted to be around or talk to *anyone* else who could understand. My away message back then for AIM was set for months to "Feeling Sad. I'll get back L8eR."

I also got a puppy. I missed Tom, so I thought a dog might fill the void. It was a temporary fix. No voids were filled, and eventually I had to give the dog to a friend. I knew I couldn't take care of her. I could barely take care of myself. I'm embarrassed to say it, but I'd wake up every morning to dog shit. Literally and figuratively. I was in an apartment on the second floor, which made it difficult to get her outside in time to go potty. I tried, but I knew she deserved a yard and a better life than I could give her. It was nice for a while, though, having the companionship, and she forced me to get outside and go for walks.

Somewhere down the line, I stopped telling people I ever had a brother. Before my brother's death, I used to always introduce myself as a twin, something I was especially proud of. That was my 'cool thing,' my 'fun fact,' my identity as I had previously known it. Whenever I'd have to introduce myself to the class and have to share a 'fun or interesting fact' about myself, I'd always lead with, "Hi, I'm Amy. I'm a twin." My Myspace account even proudly stated that in the 'About Me' section. That I had a twin brother, and that he made me snort when I laughed too hard. No longer a twin, I felt like I lost who I was. I also felt like if I talked about my younger half brothers, and not Tom, that made me an asshole. It didn't feel fair to Tom. I felt guilty about it, so I just clammed up and said nothing at all. I was still trying to process a lot and the tragic way that we had all lost Tom. I didn't want to tell people what had happened to him, and I didn't want to say it out loud because then I had to accept it. I was also afraid of other people's reactions when I told them.

I vividly remember running into an older couple at a local pub in Whitewater just a couple of months after Tom died. Tom and I would always say hi to and joke around with them, as they were regulars and very sarcastic and fun to be around. They were right up our alley. "Amy," they called from across the bar. "How the hell are ya?! We haven't seen you in a while. Where ya been, and where's that goofy-lookin' twin brother of yours?!" My heart broke into a million pieces when I had to tell them that he died. They were the first people who didn't know about it that I had to tell.

When I had to say out loud for the very first time that he

was *killed*, the horrified look on their faces said it all. It looked as if I had just told them *they* were going to die. Like I had just said, "Hey, I can see both of your futures, and when you leave this bar tonight, you will get attacked by a pack of wolves and get eaten alive and die in the most horrific way. But don't worry, you'll die together. Good luck and sayonara! I'll let your families know."

I even thought that day about changing the narrative altogether, like: 'Well, most people don't think spontaneous human combustion is real, but unfortunately it is, and that's what happened to Tom. He just kind of ignited one day and . . . poof! Up in smoke he went.' I feel like at least Tom would have thought that was hilarious. A cooler way to go out. I imagined saying this and him giving me his famous head nod and smirk from up above. Spontaneous human combustion . . . ha! Not such an unbelievable way to go when you consider the time when we were five and I thought Tom blew up.

Telling that couple was so painful that I vowed never to speak of it again if I didn't have to. I felt like, "If I tell you I have a brother, you're going to ask how he died. If you ask how he died, I'll die. I can't. I just can't." So, when people would ask me if I had any siblings, for a while I'd just respond, "Nope, only child." I feel guilty about that looking back, as I should have honored Tom and his life. It was important. He was important. It's all I could do, though, and I was just doing my best to *survive*. It wasn't until becoming a mother myself that I realized how much work goes into raising a human being, and how much each and every life matters.

I think because of the way Tom died, people's reactions to it were different. I didn't always get the same reaction that you would get, say, if someone you loved died of an illness or accident. Some people were kind of like, "Well, he put himself in that situation, he shouldn't have been buying drugs. Oh well." I even got a Myspace message from someone we went to high school with that said, "Wow, way to go, Tom. What an idiot. Sorry for your loss, Amy." It was hard to think that this was how he was going to be remembered when I knew in my heart there was just so much more. They also didn't know our background, our struggles, or Tom's pain. Some parents even used it as a story to tell their kids not to do drugs. I guess that didn't bother me as much, as at least then I felt like he didn't die in vain. I guess I just wanted Tom's story to be better. To be much, much better.

At some point, I also stopped talking about my mom as much too. My mom's loss brought up the feelings of my brother's loss, and my brother's loss brought up the feelings of my mom's loss. It was all *too* tragic, and I wanted a different story for myself. A lighter one. One that I felt fit my bubbly nature a bit more. One that came with less baggage. So I lied to people. But I lied to myself as well. It's how I learned to survive. It's how I coped.

My family also didn't talk about Tom's loss much. It became a subject that was just kind of off-limits. It was too painful for everyone, so I learned to stay quiet like everyone else. The only person I ever remember talking about my brother's death was my grandma. She was getting older, and her filter was getting less and less. I remember sometimes she would even introduce me to her friends and even strangers loudly by saying, "This is Amy. Her twin brother was murdered. Yeah, he was shot. It was hard, but here she is."

Then she would put her hand up as if she was presenting me, like Vanna White presenting the letters on *Wheel of Fortune*.

People would look aghast and stare at me uncomfortably, looking for the nearest exit sign to *run*. To be honest, it was so awkward and the look on people's faces was so priceless that I wanted to burst into laughter. I also then always felt like I had to overcompensate and talk about positive, funny things, just to balance out the conversation. Grief is an uncomfortable-enough conversation for most people, but murder is a whole other level of discomfort. So, I'd hold in any laughter the best I could, because murder and laughter go together like good food and tight jeans. They don't!

I don't like to admit this, but the other ways I coped in my early twenties was that I abused alcohol for some time and started having a controlling relationship with food. I even ended up in an abusive relationship with someone who I thought I loved and who loved me. I stayed in this relationship too long because the pain it brought me felt normal. Truth be told, it hurt much less than what I was feeling on the inside, so, in a way, it was the perfect distraction from doing the hard work of healing. After Tom's death, my need to be perfect also became much stronger. Unfortunately, in hindsight, that need for perfectionism actually stemmed from my life never actually being perfect. I didn't know that at the time, though. All I knew was that I wanted to be perfect, and I felt let down because I never could be.

Admittedly, I also pushed people away to see who would stick around. I kept a solid wall up to protect myself at all times. I even pushed away the nice guys who tried to date me because I felt undeserving of *kind* love. I felt like they were 'too good' for me. I also never felt worthy of love, and I didn't know what stability looked like because I was so used to thriving in chaos. Our nervous system will always choose familiar chaos over unfamiliar peace until we work on healing ourselves. So I lowered my standards because I felt I had too much baggage and heartache that I was carrying with me. I went for all the 'bad boys.' The good-looking ones who treated me like *shit*. Like I was just an option, because again . . . it was the perfect distraction, and I didn't think I was worthy. I also think I liked the chase because then I never had to be vulnerable.

I did fall in love with someone great once, a few years after losing Tom. I fell hard. He was nice, funny, hardworking, and kind. He made me laugh and treated me like I was a truly special find. When it came time to meet his family, though, I ruined it. I sabotaged the whole thing and pushed him away. How in the hell could I meet his family and answer any questions about myself and my story?! No way. It was too painful, so I avoided the pain at all costs. It's only now (that I'm older) that I realize anyone who didn't love me for all of me wasn't worth my time or energy. I also feel that most parents would have been kind and told me they were sorry for my losses. It's something we all inevitably face. Loss, that is. I just didn't think that at the time, and I didn't think I was worth it. So, I avoided love, truth, and vulnerability altogether. To me, it just wasn't worth it.

THE DOS AND DON'TS OF GRIEF

"Arghhhhhhhh!" I mumbled to myself as I lay in bed staring up at the fan spinning on my ceiling. Watching as the fan cord dangled back and forth while the self-loathing started to kick in, along with a pounding headache. My mouth now so dry that I could barely swallow.

I moved towards the edge of the bed to let one foot dangle off, and I placed it on the floor, hoping it would stop the room from spinning. "Please stop," I uttered under my breath in hopes the room would hear me and obey. I scanned the room corner to corner with one eye closed for better focus, hoping to find some water. I need water. Please water. No water!

Only remnants and reminders of the night before. 'Going out' clothes scattered all over the floor, shoes distanced from each other and upright (looking as though they were ready to run away from this hangover too), and a half-eaten plate of nachos sitting beside me on the nightstand.

Nachos were my go-to meal after a night of drinking. Now my cat Juno, a Persian Himalayan, was perched right next to me, staring at me with what seemed like a frown on his smushed little face. "Is he judging me?" I thought as we locked eyes for a minute until he looked down at the plate and began to graze off of last night's feast. Lick of nachos, lick of his paws, lick of nachos, lick of paws, nachos, paws, nachos, paws.

"Water!" I thought to myself again as I finally mustered up the strength to stand upright and make my way into the kitchen. I grabbed a glass out of the cabinet, turned on the faucet, and filled the glass all the way to the top. As if at any moment there could be a water shortage, and I wanted to be fully prepared. I chugged it. Just then it hit me. I needed to work this afternoon, and I needed to get a ride back to my car!

I remembered I had left my car at the local drinking establishment I went to the night before with a friend. I had asked her for a ride home, since I was in no shape to drive. Where's my phone? I grabbed my purse and dumped it on the kitchen counter, scrambling to find all the important essentials. Keys, check. Wallet, check. Phone, check. Dignity . . . nowhere in sight.

I flipped my phone open and dialed my friend's number. "Amanda," I said eagerly as she picked up her phone. "I gotta work in a few hours. Can you give me a ride back to my car?"

"Yeah," she said as she laughed on the other end. "How ya feeling?"

"Don't ask," I said. "I'll see ya soon." I flipped my phone closed and hurried to the bathroom to brush my teeth before she got to my apartment. Just then, I caught a glimpse of myself in the mirror.

"Not again," I thought to myself as I stared at my reflection. Another night of drinking. The *night* promised me I'd feel better, but the *morning* took it all back. Shame began to sink in along with frustration and anger at myself. I knew that this wasn't the way to handle my grief, but my twenty-four-year-old self grasped onto what was easiest . . . which was trying to numb the pain. I was on an unintentional path to self-destruction, and deep down I knew it. The abusive boyfriend, the alcohol, the late nights out. I knew I could do better. I knew this couldn't be it.

I learned pretty quickly that alcohol and grief don't mix well. While it might help for a little while, the pain will show back up in the morning times two. I also learned that people's reactions to your loss shouldn't deter you from speaking about it. It became evident to me that since I was a people pleaser, I didn't want to open up about my hardships because it made *other* people feel awkward. Since death, loss, and grief can be socially uncomfortable topics, I made sure I didn't speak about them much. That when I did, it was only after a night of drinking so I didn't care about others' reactions. I'm not sure why I cared so much about making others uncomfortable. Why didn't I care more about myself?

In hindsight, maybe it's because people can also say some pretty ridiculous responses to others' pain and loss. Here are some of my personal favorites, in no particular order: "Holy shit," "I don't even know what to say," "Yikes," "That sucks," "Oh boy," "How are you still here?" "They're in a better place anyway," "I can't relate," "I've never lost anybody . . . THANK GOD!" "That's a lot," "You gotta be strong and get over it," "What doesn't kill you makes you stronger," oh, and I even had someone pretend once that they didn't hear me. Like pause, make brief eye contact, and completely change the subject. I think because grief reminds people of their own demise, and some people just don't want to hear about it. Grief is a part of life, though. It's beautiful, chaotic, and messy. Why can't we just leave it the way it is?

The *best* way that I've had someone respond is with "I'm here." Two words. Two simple words with a lot of impact. I think it also helps a lot when people give you space to talk about your grief. Or ask about the person who died. Who were they, what did they like to do, *why* were they important to you? NOT how they died. That topic is saved for people who are close. Family and close friends. Strangers who ask that can come across as being nosy or searching for ways they can save their own life. Prevent their own demise.

My takeaway on grief:

DO: Lean into your feelings and allow yourself to feel the pain.

DON'T: Worry about what others think or try and make them comfortable at the expense of making yourself uncomfortable.

DO: Give yourself grace. You'll need it.

DON'T: Be afraid to seek help for your pain.

DO: Talk about your loved ones you've lost. It's important.

DON'T: Numb the pain. It's there. Honor it.

DO: Spend time around others who allow you a space to grieve.

It took me a while to learn these things and to learn that in order to deal with your grief, you have to sit with it. You have to be-friend it, nurture it. Treat it like it matters . . . because it does. Oh, and if you ever want to console someone else in their grief, never say any sentence that starts with "At least." For me, it wasn't until my grandpa passed away that everything came to a screeching halt. I had no choice but to seek help. I was backed into a corner with no escape. Because grieving anyone can bring up the grief of everyone. The abusive relationship I was in fell apart, and then losing my grandpa was the final straw. In full transparency, I also started taking an antidepressant. It helped.

RESILIENCE

I never knew what the word resilience meant until my grandpa said it to me before his death. I was twenty-four when Grandpa fell ill with cancer. Each family member got to say our goodbyes one at a time. I thought long and hard about what I was going to say, as Grandpa was a role model to me my entire life. He was always there when I needed him (and I appreciated his consistency, something I didn't always have much of growing up).

In the fourth grade, we were assigned to write a paper on our hero. Most students in my class chose famous people: presidents, celebrities, and popular musicians. I wrote mine about him. I remember calling him that afternoon to interview him for my paper. In my nine-year-old mind, I needed to be professional about this. I took it *very* seriously. I had a list of questions written out with my pen to paper, as I wedged the phone between my shoulder and ear. I cleared my throat; I was ready. When I got him on the other line and told him what the paper was about, I could hear his voice crack a little. He was choked up because out of all people, I chose him.

He chatted up a storm that day, and I scribbled everything down on my paper as rapidly as I could, so I didn't miss a thing. He told me about how he served in World War II and received a medal for being a sharpshooter; how he lived in Burbank, California, just after the war and worked as a concrete finisher; how he started Concrete Placement Company when he returned back home; how he helped build the home he raised his family in; how he worked on the weekends to build the duplex he and my grandma eventually rented out; and how being a dad was his greatest accomplishment. He was also fond of being a grandfather too, he told me, and felt such joy teaching me and all my cousins the important lessons he'd learned throughout his life.

He said he loved watching us all grow up, and my childhood memories confirm this. Grandma was always making the house smell like a home by cooking the big Italian meals for family dinners, but he was the one who initiated the fun things like hiding money in plastic, colored Easter eggs for our yearly epic 'Cousin Easter Egg Hunt,' taking us fishing, and playing board games with us, one of which he created entirely himself. I can't remember the name of it, but it had all these cool, elaborate pieces and something to do with ships. He even welded all the little pieces for it himself.

During our call, he told me that he always felt an innate responsibility to take good care of my grandma, which he did. I'd give him an A+ for effort. He met my grandma (Harriet) decades earlier through her older brother Gio, short for Giovanni. They became friends, but didn't end up dating until after he returned home from the war. He started taking care of my grandma way back then. Grandma was the youngest of five. She was ten years younger than my grandfather. This age gap was not uncommon back then. In fact, my grandfather's father was fifteen years older than his mother.

Grandma's family was very Italian. Think Sopranos Italian without the illegal mob activity. Her father was actually born in Italy. Every last name on both her mother's and father's side of the family ended in a vowel. Descenzo, Italiano, Congemi. Her great-grandparents even had Italian first names, Vincenzo and Concetta. Grandma's talking often sounded like yelling, but she graciously pointed out (when we traveled to Italy together in my mid-twenties) that this was not an uncommon trait for Italians. She made me aware that she, like many of her ancestors, was just speaking passionately. Grandpa understood this as well.

When my grandparents first met, my grandma was still in high school and confided in my grandfather that she didn't want to finish her schooling because she didn't have any nice clothes to wear. She told him that she was embarrassed and that the other girls in her high school were all fashionably dressed. She felt subpar, inadequate, and it made her feel insecure inside. She told him that she didn't want to go back. He made her promise to go back and graduate, though. He reminded her that education was very important. He then went out and bought her a new, beautiful cashmere sweater for every day of the week. It's been said that she ended up being one of the best-dressed girls in her graduating class. She also graduated *with honors*.

Grandma tended to worry a lot. She once told me that when she was little, she would stare out the front window of the house waiting for her mother to return home from work, feeling lonely and worrying herself until she was sick to her stomach. She would pick a topic and hyper-focus on it. She has done this ever since I can remember. Someone once told her that if she didn't eat enough carrots, she would go blind. She said when she was young she worried about that, among other things. She knew it was ludicrous, but she couldn't help it. She just had a busy mind. I think when she met Grandpa, though, he made her feel safe. He made her feel loved. He quieted her mind. He was always her rock and felt like home to her, and she needed that.

When I finally walked in the den and sat next to Grandpa on his favorite, worn-in, brown, leather couch, I looked at him with a forced smile and tears streaming down my face. My grandfather did not like to see anyone hurting, especially his own family. I know he felt my pain through that bear hug I gave him. He quickly grabbed a handful of the Lemonhead candies that were sitting on the TV stand beside him, alongside some losing lottery tickets he had already scratched off. He put the candies in the front pocket of my purse. That was his way of trying to lighten the mood. He then looked at me before I could say a word and told me he'd always been proud of me for being *resilient*. I had heard that word before but was never quite sure of its full meaning until that day. In my mind, I knew it meant something along the lines of *strong*, and now I was sobbing. My neck was also broken out in hives, as it often does when I become unsettled.

By this time, I had already experienced the loss and hardship of losing my mom and brother, and Grandpa was there to bear witness to it all. My heart still aches to know that he was a spectator to all the devastating, distressing events. He knew the pain I carried around with me each and every day, yet I still tried my best to forge ahead and make something of myself. Maybe because I knew my hero was also watching. Grandpa stood up in court to address my brother's killer just one year prior. When he was elderly and sick with bone cancer. He walked up to the stand to talk about Tom with dignity, dressed nicely, with his shirt perfectly tucked into his pants and a comb neatly placed in his back pocket. He did it for the sake of his family, and for his family's name and legacy. A name that was carried on through him, but would now no longer carry on. He did it because it was the right thing to do.

I looked at Grandpa and gave him another big hug. An unspoken goodbye hug. By this time, I was sweating and crying so hard it made it hard to even speak. I then made him promise to say hello to some special people in heaven first thing when he got there. "Grandpa, you promise me?" I asked. He knew who I was talking about, and he promised me that he would. In my heart, in that moment, I silently promised him to never stop being resilient. I also kept those Lemonheads in my purse for close to two years after he passed. Whenever I missed him, I'd hold them in my hand, close my eyes, and remember him.

I also studied the word resilient so I could keep my promise to him.

Resilient. Characterized or marked by resilience, such as tending to recover from or adjust easily to misfortune or change. Being resilient does not mean a person doesn't experience stress, emotional upheaval, and suffering. Resilience involves the ability to work through emotional pain and suffering.

Resilient (adjective): The ability to withstand adversity and bounce back from difficult life events.

HEALING IS MESSY

It was really important for me to keep my promise to my grandpa. After all, he was the most loyal person I knew. Right down to making me his famous bologna sandwich every time I saw him, to putting ten-dollar bills in my hand during my college 'poor years,' and insisting I 'never tell Grandma.' So after he passed, I sought out therapy for myself. I googled "anxiety therapists" and a nice-looking blonde woman's picture and email address popped up.

I wrote and rewrote my email to her several times. Each time trying to sound more professional and 'less crazy.' The truth is, I just wanted to email "Hellllppppppppppppppppp! I can't take it anymore. Something's wrong!" At that point, I was having frequent panic attacks and horrible nightmares, but I didn't know what was happening. I would get triggered by something (maybe a song or an image on the news) and my heart would race, my palms would sweat, and I felt like I couldn't catch my breath no matter how many deep breaths I took. Sometimes I'd even hold my breath, hoping it would stop or restart or jump-start. Anything to help catch my breath.

People on the outside didn't know how much I was struggling on the inside. Everything looked okay. I had graduated
from college and was the first grandchild in my family to set that
precedent. I had my own cute little apartment and was support-
ing myself. I had completed two internships at notable TV stations and one at a local radio station, and I was working a caregiving job near my apartment while sending out resume tapes in
my field. I was hanging out with friends, going out in the city,
going through the motions. Everything looked fine, but I knew
I needed to talk to someone again. I was beginning to crack, and
I knew it was time.

A few days later, the nice-looking lady finally got back to
me and reassured me she could help. Hearing that felt like I had
finally come up for air after swimming underwater. I paid for
therapy all out of pocket. I wasn't making much money at the
time, but I reminded myself it was an investment that would pay
off in the end. I knew it was something I needed (especially if I
ever wanted to start a family of my own one day), and I liked my
therapist from the first moment we met.

She was motherly, and, as I mentioned before, I was always
looking for that in others. Her voice was soothing, and her eyes
were kind. She also let her curly hair flow freely and a little friz-
zly, which made her less intimidating. We even looked a little
alike. She was tall, thin, and blonde. She believed in holistic
remedies (along with traditional medicine), and she made me
feel safe, so I bared my soul.

One session, she encouraged me to sign up for a weekend intensive therapy session. She promised that if I did, she would give
me a scholarship for it. I wasn't keen on the idea, but I also wasn't
one to turn down free money. It would be three long days. Friday

evening, and all day Saturday and Sunday. I would only go home to sleep, then would come right back. We would even eat there.

I told my boyfriend at the time I was out of town with my family with no cell service. I laughed so many times thinking to myself how funny it would be to change my voicemail. "Hey, it's Amy. So sorry I can't get to the phone right now, I'm just in twenty hours of intensive therapy for being a little cray cray at the moment, but leave a message and I'll call you back when I'm sane."

While there, we all focused on our trauma. Some people there were even war veterans. Others had also experienced huge, tragic losses. We had to get up in front of the room to share our story and tell how it made us feel. I volunteered *last*, and I secretly hoped they would forget about me. I hoped that if I stayed quiet enough and still enough in the very back row, they'd skip right over me. I even shrunk down a little. They didn't, and when it was my turn to go up there, I had a flashback of standing at the front of Mrs. Stillman's room. Only this time, there was no Tommy to hide behind. I felt naked and exposed. *Again.*

They asked me to reenact my last day with Tommy. I couldn't believe it was happening. I had to pick one male student from the class and pretend it was him. Then we had to recreate our last conversation together, only this time I could say goodbye. I could tell him all the things I didn't get to say to him before he died. I searched the room for a person who reminded me most of him. It was a tough call, as there were only two males, but I chose the older gentleman (in his early seventies) who had been cracking jokes the whole weekend and who had kind eyes. He seemed harmless enough. He also appeared honored that I chose him.

He walked up proudly to the front of the room and sat next

to me in a chair. I stared at him for a little while until realizing that I was the one who had to initiate this 'skit.' "You've got to be kidding?!" I thought to myself, but once we started reenacting that day, it truly felt like I was back in time. I told him I was sorry I went to the gym the morning he was killed. That I wished I had stayed home to spend the morning with him. That I wished I'd taken care of him because he was sick with a cold that day, and that's always made me sad to think about. That I was sorry I complained of his strong cologne smell when I got back from the gym that morning. The truth was I loved that smell because it represented my twin and favorite person.

I told him I was sorry he was killed. That he didn't deserve that, and that I really hope he didn't feel much pain in his final moments. That it was quick. That I miss him every day, and that I would give anything to have him back. That most days I feel lost, and like I'm just pretending to live life. Also, that I keep seeing people that look like him everywhere, and I feel like he's pranking me. That he *has* to be pranking me.

After all the words came out of my mouth, I sobbed uncontrollably. I forgot I was even standing in front of a room of people. I even forgot where I was for a bit. I had never felt so vulnerable in my life. Then I looked around the room, and everyone had warm, compassionate looks on their faces. Some others were crying with me. A lady even came up to me and handed me a pin. It was a pin she had received when she served in the war. "I want you to have this," she said. "I want you to remember how brave you are, and that you are never alone." She insisted I have it, despite me saying I just couldn't take it. I hugged her and tucked it into my pocket. I still have that pin, and I still think of that sweet lady today.

After this, I was encouraged to let out a scream. This was the hardest assignment for me to do. I don't like being angry. People always ask if I'm angry, and honestly, that emotion makes me very uncomfortable. It's never been who I am, but I followed what I was told to do.

The first scream I let out was dainty. It was soft, and I was very aware that everyone was looking at me, so I didn't want to scream. "Louder," I was told. I screamed a little louder. "Amy, how did you feel the day you found out your brother was murdered?" Scream like that! "AHHHHHHHHHHHHHHHHHHHHHH." I let out the ugliest scream you have ever heard. I'm pretty sure it was the loudest noise that has ever come out of my body, and then I immediately fell to the floor, sobbing into my hands. Thankfully everyone embraced me, and I was encouraged to 'just rest' after that. I think I took a nap on a bean bag chair in the corner the rest of the day.

After that intensive weekend of therapy, I continued regular in-office therapy after that. That same therapist introduced me to the concept of holistic therapies. Reiki, acupuncture, yoga, meditation, etc. She also encouraged me to start journaling again (which I had given up after Tom was killed). It was just too painful, and writing it down only solidified his death. So I'd stopped doing the one thing that had helped me overcome my previous loss. She encouraged me to take it slow. To start by writing one paragraph at a time, or even simple words or thoughts about how I was feeling. She also asked me to write a letter to "little Amy" from "big Amy." She told me to do this using my left hand. "You will be surprised at what comes out, Amy," she said.

I laughed so hard the way home from therapy the day she

told me this. This sounded like complete Freudian trickery. If the same person is writing a letter to the same person, what new could possibly come up? "Hey Amy, it's Amy. How are you!? I'm good. How are you?! Good. Wow!" I couldn't even muster up her assignment for around two weeks. I waited to do my 'homework' until hours before our next therapy session. Of course I was going to do it, as I've always been very type A and wouldn't *not* do an assignment tasked to me. I decided, though, it would be on my terms.

What came up was a whole lot more than I ever imagined. I was terribly sad and felt let down by those around me. I felt let down and that Mom and Tom in a way left me. I guess in my "little Amy" mind I felt like they had a choice. I was sad Mom and Dad divorced. Some small part of me felt like if they had pulled it together, everything would be different and maybe Mom and Tom would still be here. I guess I was mad at Dad too. I felt like I was always chasing him and vying for his attention. I also realized that I felt like I had to be perfect even as a child. Like Tom could 'act out,' but I had to 'listen.' It was a lot to take in, but she helped me slowly unpack my trauma one brick at a time. We worked together for quite some time. I also later found out that using your less dominant hand to write is known to be a great way to access the voice of your inner child. And let's face it, there's a little child in all of us that needs to be let out and heard.

Around that time, I also started to get really into holistic practices like yoga, acupuncture, meditation, mindfulness, massage therapy, talk therapy, and Reiki to work on finding healing. It helped. I wanted to heal myself because not only did I realize that I deserved it, and owed it to myself, but I wanted to *stop* the generational trauma. I wanted to lay it to rest the best I could. I started to eat healthier too, as I studied the correlation between the mind/gut connection. I began working out, journaling, and drinking more water instead of alcohol. I listened to videos and read books about healing and trauma written by authors who inspired me. Any and all forms of holistic healing I was interested in and willing to try. I even did a modeling job for deprivation float tanks in return for a year of free floats. That was a peaceful and fun year.

I learned the importance of showing up for myself. I began working on forgiving myself for some of the poor ways that I had handled Mom and Tom's losses throughout the years. I owed that to myself too. Sometime around then, I also decided that I wanted to help others. My empathy for pain and struggle became even stronger through all of my experiences. Lastly, although I graduated from college with a degree in broadcast journalism, I switched gears altogether. I made up my mind that I wanted to help better people's lives instead of reporting on them. I changed career goals from TV and radio to social services. A friend of mine at the time said there was a case manager opening at the company he worked for, and he thought I would be a strong candidate for the job.

"Well, what do I do?" I asked.

"You help people," he said. "You have a bachelor's degree and experience working with the less fortunate from when you worked at different group homes. And you genuinely care about people, Amy, which is what really matters. You'd be a fit."

So I applied, and I got the job. Just like when I worked at my first caregiving job in Whitewater, I loved it. I felt at home, and I felt like I was truly making a difference. Yes, I saw pain, poverty, sadness, and struggle. But I could actually 'do' something about it this time, and *that* made me happy. I worked in this field for around eight years until I had my daughter. If you've struggled in any capacity and seen life's hardships, helping others is the most direct way to experience less pain. It can truly be healing as it can take you out of your own pain and help you feel less alone. I also got to see all different walks of life, all different struggles, and all different backgrounds. It was humbling, and it reminded me that we all have obstacles we have to overcome. We all have pain and heartache, and we all need a little *hope* and a helping hand sometimes.

I also decided that I wanted to teach yoga to others. Yoga has been so helpful to me in working through the pain and trauma stored in my own body. I wanted to help others release their trauma and feel better physically and mentally too. So, I completed two hundred hours of yoga teacher training at a local yoga studio to become a certified yoga instructor. I also completed a basic Reiki certification as well to understand the concept of energy and healing. I've taught yoga now for around eight years. I learned throughout this process that we have four trauma responses: fight, flight, freeze, or fawn. Yoga and mindfulness have helped me to identify when I'm in one of these four responses and have helped me to work through it.

I still have days in which I lean into one of these responses, though. The one I lean into the most is *freeze*. If my body is telling me it can't do anything at the moment and it needs to relax, I usually honor this response and allow myself to shut down for a bit. Being a yoga instructor, I've learned the importance of listening to my body. I've been known to shut down for even a day, as I do consider this response (for me, at least) a reset. I always just promise myself that tomorrow I will get up and try again.

Being outdoors and traveling has also been healing for me. Whenever I travel, I tuck a photo of my mom and brother in the front pocket of my suitcase. It feels, in a sense, like I'm taking them with me. Taking them both to see some of the cool places they never got to see in this life. And you don't have to travel far to bring a little solitude. I've learned just being outside in nature is healing just the same. It's a space to connect, reset, breathe, get away from the hustle and bustle. Maybe even talk to our loved ones who have passed. Like a spiritual safe haven, and I believe they can always hear us.

I've saved up and traveled to a few different countries. I even traveled to Bali once, and got to meet a traditional healer. Balinese healers are known for healing physical, mental, and spiritual pain. I don't exactly remember what he was doing during our healing session (perhaps something with reflexology), but he told me I look young, yet I have an old heart, and that I've experienced immense sadness. He then pushed on my feet on a pressure point for as long as he could and released, and I felt better. Maybe it was just in my head, but my physical body did feel lighter. There was definitely a spiritual magic about it. It was a cool experience.

When I traveled to Italy in my late twenties, I also found a lot of healing. I remember being in Siena and sitting on some cathedral steps, staring up at the sky. It was eerily quiet and still, and I was completely immersed in a different, beautiful culture. I recall thinking about how I so badly wanted my mom to see this. How I wanted her to experience such a beautiful place, and how she never got to and never would. In a way, I even felt guilty inside about that. Just then, a flock of birds flew above me in a synchronized fashion, looking so peaceful, beautiful, and at ease.

The whole city seemed to stand still. It was really quiet, calm, and peaceful. It sounds cliché, but I felt her presence so strongly that day. It was at that moment that I realized that she *was* with me. That she'd always be with me.

From that moment on, I truly started to believe that we *will* meet our lost loved ones again and that we owe it to them to live our best life. For us and for *them*. That we carry them with us, and that wherever we go, they go. I find comfort in that idea, and I don't think our lost loved ones are ever far. I even find myself channeling my mom sometimes, singing loudly throughout the house, being goofy like she was, saying things she would have said, and rooting for all the underdogs in life. We can always remember our loved ones' best qualities and carry them on in ourselves.

Every day is a work in progress, but I realize I'm worth it. We all are.

HOPE

Hope is loving even when you're scared of losing. Hope is committing even when you're scared of commitment. Hope is taking a chance when you're scared of failing. Hope is seeing the good in people when it's easier to see the bad. Hope is carrying on even when it seems too scary and impossible to do so. Hope is choosing life over death, love over fear. Hope is finding out that your mother's heart gave someone else life. Hope is a feeling of trust. A trust that things will always get better. Hope is all we have.

After several years of working on healing, I finally met someone I wanted to take a real chance on love with. He was different. There was comfort with Dan. No questioning things, no not answering my phone calls, no chasing, no dodging, no riding my bike to the bars trying to find him, no expectations of me, no intentional pain inflicted, he just *was*. He was just always there . . . by my side.

There's a children's book called *The Rabbit Listened* by Cori Doerrfeld. I've read it to my daughter before. It's about a rabbit who sits near a grieving child every day until he feels better. The rabbit shows up day after day, sitting right next to him. Meeting him exactly where he is. There's no telling him how to handle things, blaming him for the way he handles things, or expecting him to be better. He just listens and waits. To me, Dan has always been the rabbit. In the most beautiful way, he shows up patiently and sits by my side. With absolutely no motive but to be there. Next to me.

It took a while for me to accept this kind of love, but I finally did. I remember telling my therapist that I wasn't sure about this. "It feels weird," I said. She looked me directly in the eyes and said, "Amy, it's time to try a different shoe on and get used to it." I knew what she was saying. Enough inflicting pain on myself as a distraction. It was the last card again in the deck that I had left to play. So I slowly set it down and stopped playing the game.

He was kind and patient. He gave me the consistency I needed and always longed for. He proposed, and we married, and now we have a daughter, Penelope. She's the light of my life. My biggest joy, my greatest accomplishment. She's beautiful, smart, and funny, and when I look at her sometimes, I see so much of her uncle Tommy—the best parts of her uncle Tommy. Often when I think of him, I think that he would have made a hell of an uncle. She makes me laugh like he did, and she's *very* smart like he was. Clever and sometimes too smart for her own good. She's the new yin to my yang, and it wasn't until she was born and placed in my arms for the first time that the hole in my heart became smaller.

I have to be honest, though. I still have some lasting effects from trauma left in me to this day. Some ways I cope when things get hard. I've accepted them, and embraced that I am who I am. Here they are in no particular order:

I still tend to check in on people I love a lot. Not as much as I used to, but I still have a little hypervigilance left in me. I guess when people tell me I worry a little too much, I say they've never lost a life they've loved.

I'm still the go-to person in my family when someone needs something. It's in my nature to want to help, but I'm working on finding ways to put myself first and set healthy boundaries. With practice, this has become a little easier to do.

I'm a bit of a minimalist. Losing people has shown me that material things matter *the least* in this life, and experiences matter the most. I've sold and/or donated a *lot* of stuff. Sometimes my home can even look a little too basic or staged. I just don't want my life to be about collecting things, but rather about experiencing *life*. We don't leave this world with material things, but rather a full heart. I'm also pretty mindful of what I purchase. I've taught my daughter this too, as I think it's important. We even have an 'adventure fund' where we take money out every weekend to go experience new and *fun adventures*. It's one of our favorite traditions.

Another quirk I have is that I clean a lot. In my mind, when everything in the outside world turns to shit, it makes me happy that my house is clean. To this day, perfect vacuum lines and a lit candle make me feel completely content. It's a way I sort through any messy feelings inside. Last, I tend to schedule doctors' appointments pretty quickly after learning that someone doesn't feel well. If I don't, I'll get in my head about it, so whether it's me or someone I love, an appointment will be scheduled. I guess because my losses were sudden, I feel that if a doctor can do a 'once-over,' maybe it'll save a life.

I can also be a bit 'overly' optimistic and 'too nice' sometimes.

Heart emoji here, smile there, kind gesture here, sprinkled in with a positive quote there. I once heard this quote, "Never mistake my kindness for weakness," and it resonated with me. I wish more people could remember it's a strength to be kind to others when you're hurting. It's a strength to stay positive and hopeful when your world gets hard. It's a strength to show vulnerability when you've been deeply hurt. It's a strength to remember that the world is hard enough, you don't need to be a part of the problem. This doesn't mean I don't have bad days, because I do. Especially around hard anniversaries. I just try to be kind, because I know pain, and we all have it.

Auntie Mary has since passed away too. She passed away unexpectedly two and a half years ago. She's another one of the *good ones* that is gone too soon. Another one from the old 'Frame Avenue Crew.' Losing Aunt Mary was like losing another mom. Our relationship was so beautiful, and losing her shook me. However, I handled this grief differently. I say this because I've learned that grief is *okay*. It's normal, it's *healthy*.

The difference with this loss was I leaned into it this time. My previous losses taught me about grief, so I leaned hard. I wanted to make her proud and be honest with myself, so I gave myself permission to experience ALL my feelings. I let myself be sad when I wanted to. I gave up alcohol for a year and a half and counting to allow myself to *feel* all the feelings. I cried and even sobbed when I needed to. I lay down to rest when my daughter lay down. I talked about her to anyone who would listen. I talked to her. I cherished our beautiful bond. It still hurts, but I don't run from it, and I don't want to run from it. Again, I've learned grief is just love disguised. We owe it to ourselves and those we've lost to grieve them. It's okay. Grief is okay!

My daughter did get to meet her, and Aunt Mary is the main reason I've faced my past head-on and written this book. Aunt Mary adored Penelope, and Penelope adored her. My daughter even called her Grandma Mary, which she had said was the greatest gift I could have ever given her. Being a grandma, that is. It was the least I could do for all she did for me. Aside from that, my mom would have been so happy about that gift too. Auntie Mary's belief in me throughout the years kept me afloat and helped me to believe in myself. I would not be the woman I am today if it wasn't for her. She taught me to stop always waiting for the other shoe to drop. That even when you experience pain, it's okay to find and celebrate the good.

She also taught me to not anticipate the bad, because what goes up must always come down. She'd say, "Amy, celebrate the good while it's here. Soak it all in, and relish in it. Don't wait for the bad to come. Life's too short." In essence, what she was saying was that everything is temporary, so enjoy each moment while it's here. I'm thankful that she got to see me settle into the life I have now. I feel blessed because I have an amazing family, a beautiful daughter, a nice place to call home, and wonderful friends. I've also always been able to find my purpose by listening to my heart. I treasure it all and try not to take anything for granted. I've learned that this is the stuff in life that matters. It's the only thing that matters. This is the *good* stuff.

As for my dad, we lean on each other now. He watches out for me, and I watch out for him. He's become one of my *favorite* people. Through his hardships, he's changed a lot. He's grown a lot. He's also always in my corner and my biggest fan. Even while writing this book, he told me, "Amy, don't worry about what you say about me, my lovely daughter, speak your truth.

Always speak your truth. It's what's most important." His doctor's office receptionist told me once that he comes in early just to brag about his daughter. He even brought in my modeling portfolio once to show everybody. I laughed so hard when they told me this, but it's comforting to know he's always rooting for me, even when I don't know about it. My younger brothers are too, and I'm their biggest cheerleader, just like my dad is for me.

Maybe it's his humor, or maybe it's because we went through a whole other life together. A life that seems like forever ago, but one that shaped us both nevertheless. It made us who we are today. My daughter loves my dad (Papa G), and I rely on him to share stories about the 'good old days' on Frame Avenue with her. Also, to tell Penelope—Petey, as he calls her—about her funny uncle and beautiful grandma up in heaven. I rely on him today to help me keep their spirits alive.

All of the loss and heartache I've experienced have also made me more empathetic to other people's pain. Almost to a fault sometimes. I've always felt like I could feel other people's pain and sadness deeply, and I've always felt a responsibility to help others feel better. Now I experience it even more. My dad likes to remind me of a time when I was younger (around eight or so at the time) and he took me to the mall. While there, I immediately spotted one of those claw machines full of stuffed animals, the ones where the claw has to be in an almost impossible spot to actually pick one up. He said I begged him for more and more quarters until I finally won a stuffed animal. He spent about ten dollars on that claw machine that day (forty or more quarters, if you're counting).

According to my dad, once I had the stuffed animal in hand, I then walked it over and gave it to an elderly woman in a wheelchair who had been watching me inquisitively the entire time. As soon as I handed her the stuffed bunny, she got the biggest smile on her face. She also then went over and said something to my dad, but he never told me what she said. He said in return, it gave him a smile and a sense of pride too. He reminds me of this story from time to time, so I don't harden when the world tries to harden me. He tells me in hopes that I remain the same, uninfluenced, unphased person I was when I was little. The person I was born as.

I've discovered that when you find yourself in the depths of despair (where it feels hard to go on even one day longer), give it one more try. Take one more step. Put one foot in front of the other, and keep trying. Through the good, the bad, the ugly, the gains, the losses, the births, the deaths, the trials, the tribulations. Embrace it all. It's all a part of our existence, and I've come to learn it all matters. It's all a part of our story, and we should embrace our whole story and try our best to heal our traumas. We owe it to ourselves, our kids, and future generations.

Through all of this, though, if you ask me how I got here, and how I don't let the world harden me when life knocks me down, how I survived when I felt like my dreams were absolutely crushed, I will tell you. While different therapies and finding patience with myself helped a lot, there was one thing that helped me to survive and persevere even more. That is, *hope*. That's why I wanted to share *my* story.

Remember the hope glasses from the beginning of my story? How I still find a way to wear them proudly no matter how busted, hazy, and fragmented they've become? It's because hope is all we've got in this life. It's all we have in times of despair, challenge, defeat, loss, grief, and heartache. It's the only thing that will carry us forward when we feel like we just can't go on any longer. It's the only thing that truly matters.

And as for Christmases now, they are still my favorite even though they look a little different these days. I celebrate them with my own family now. I love seeing the magic and hope through my daughter's eyes. We listen to music and dance around the decorated tree like I did when I was young. We've also started our own traditions, like drinking hot chocolate when we open gifts, and staying in our pajamas all day long. I soak up these moments as much as I possibly can. I now know they're what's most important. And if you listen closely, on Christmas morning, you might even hear a little Fleetwood Mac playing in the background.

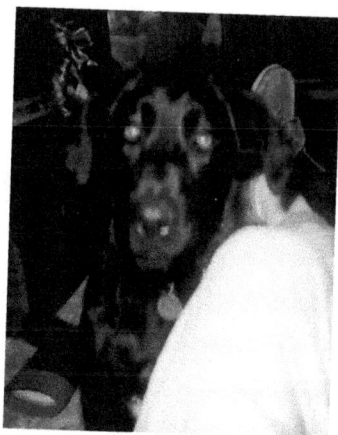

In the still of the darkness, sitting only with the moon
Always remember, I sit beside you
& when you can't even bear to face another long day
Because the world seems only hopeless and gray
Look around you, my love, I'm in everything you see
I'll always be with you, and you with me
Put your feet on the ground and live out your dreams,
Because nothing is ever as long as it seems